THE CANADIAN PRESS

ONE HUNDRED GREATEST
CANADIAN SPORTS MOMENTS

ONE HUNDRED GREATEST

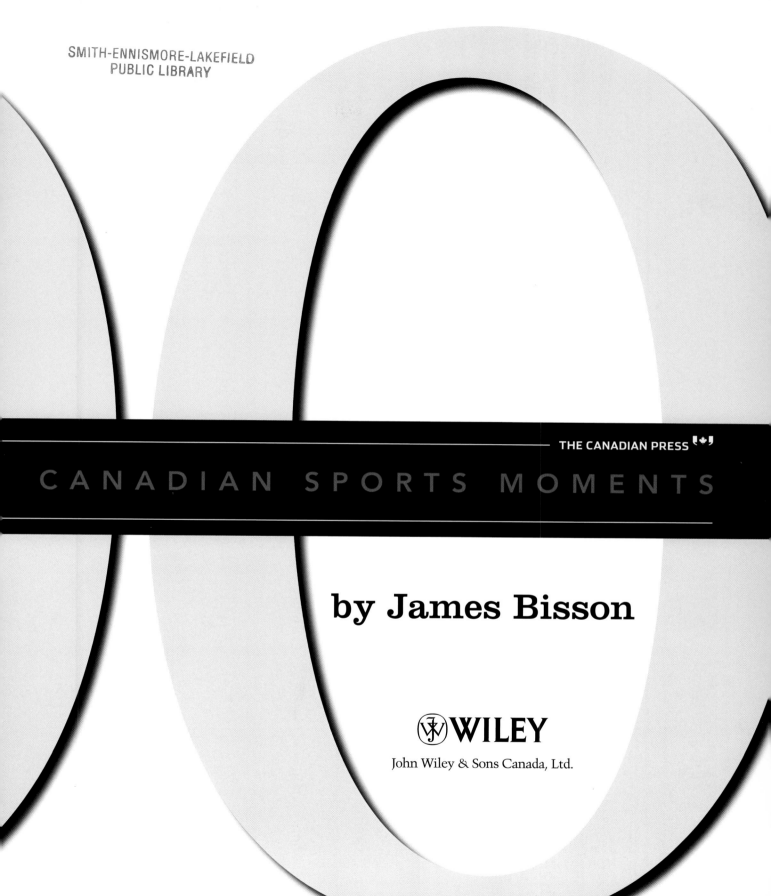

THE CANADIAN PRESS

CANADIAN SPORTS MOMENTS

by James Bisson

WILEY

John Wiley & Sons Canada, Ltd.

Library and Archives Canada Cataloguing in Publication Data

Bisson, James, 1977–

One hundred greatest moments in Canadian sports history / James Bisson.

ISBN 978-0-470-15543-1

    1. Sports—Canada—History. 2. Athletes—Canada—History. I. Title. II. Title: One hundred greatest moments in Canadian sports history.

GV585.B58 2008   796.0971   C2008-902158-4

Production Credits
Cover design: Adrian So
Interior design and typesetting: Adrian So
Cover photos: See page 160
Printer: Quebecor—Taunton

John Wiley & Sons Canada, Ltd.
6045 Freemont Blvd.
Mississauga, Ontario
L5R 4J3

Printed in the United States

1 2 3 4 5 QW 12 11 10 09 08

Dedicated to my father, Roger Bisson,
for always letting me read the sports section first

CONTENTS

Courtesy of TSN

FOREWORD by Brian Williams

OVER THE YEARS, some of the defining moments in our country's history have come from sport and those competing in sport. Sport, of course, must always be kept in perspective—but having said that, it has played a prominent role in Canadian society.

Stephen Brunt wrote the following in *The Globe and Mail* while covering the 2008 European soccer championship in Switzerland:

"Sport is always a way to get a read on a place. It isn't everything, it isn't definitive, it doesn't speak to subtleties or complexities. But understanding what game matters most, being around for singular sporting moments, ought to at least provide a clue. And no, Canada is not just hockey, but an outsider seeking to know something of the nation and its people could do worse than starting with a day in September of 1972."

He is absolutely right on.

Yes, Canada and Canadian sport are more than hockey, but it is most often hockey—especially international hockey—that spurs fans, writers, and broadcasters to speak of the indomitable Canadian spirit and our ability to overcome adversity.

I was in the Luzhniki Arena in Moscow in September of 1972 and witnessed a small group of outnumbered Canadian fans make such noise and show such pride that it stunned the sold-out Soviet crowd, which included Leonid Brezhnev. Ask most Canadians of a certain age and they will tell you where they were that day in 1972 when Paul Henderson scored his historic goal.

Beginning with the Canada–Russia series in 1972, I have been fortunate to have witnessed many of the major sporting events that have helped to define our country.

There's Ben Johnson in Seoul in 1988, becoming the first Canadian to win the men's 100-metre event at the Olympics since Vancouver's Percy Williams won in Amsterdam in 1928. And of course, after his gold medal was taken away, there was the very public Dubin Inquiry into the use of steroids in sport. The fact that the inquiry was even held, while other nations stuck their heads in the sand and refused to deal with the problem of drugs in sport, speaks volumes about the beliefs and standards in this country.

There's Donovan Bailey, winning and keeping the gold medal for the men's 100-metre in Atlanta—and the historic win by the Canadian men's

foreword continued

4 x 100–metre relay team one week later. Consider the 2006 Winter Olympics in Turin, where 16 of 24 Canadian medals were won by women, and where, at the closing ceremony, the mayor of the next host city, Vancouver, was confined to a wheelchair. These events speak volumes about our nation and the opportunities afforded to us all.

The great thing about sport is that it arouses passion and initiates great debate. Passionate debate is often the result of watching a particular sporting event or discussing the accomplishments of a certain athlete. A good debate forces people to think and hopefully become involved in reading and research, as a good debate is the product of knowledge and solid research. As Howard Cosell once told me, "The best ad-libs are rehearsed."

When I first read the manuscript for this book and looked at the top-100 list, I said, "Wait just a minute. What about the events and athletes that were *not* included?"

There's England's Roger Bannister and Australia's John Landy running the miracle sub–four-minute mile at the British Empire Games in Vancouver in 1952.

There's Phil Edwards winning a total of five Olympic medals in track at the 1928 Olympics in Amsterdam, the 1932 Games in Los Angeles, and the 1936 Games in Berlin. And like the great American Jesse Owens, Edwards was able to further destroy Hitler's myth of white superiority.

There's Dave Steen winning a bronze medal in the decathlon in Seoul in 1988. That is the only Canadian medal ever won in that event, and it was unfortunately overshadowed by the events surrounding Ben Johnson.

There's Willie O'Ree breaking the colour barrier in the NHL, and the many accomplishments of Doug Flutie in the CFL.

Wondering why these events and athletes were not included is part of the appeal of this book. It will force you to think and debate and to realize what a rich sports history we have in this country. You will not only enjoy and debate the events and the athletes selected, you hopefully, as I did, will have your memory refreshed and learn as you read about each particular event and athlete.

As Canadians, too often we fail to appreciate and learn about our history. James Bisson and his panel of experts have taken a wonderful look at our sports history—and this book will help every reader do the same.

Brian Williams
CTV Olympic Host

PREFACE

A GOOD SPORTS DEBATE isn't hard to find.

Every city and town in Canada has hosted lively discussions about which teams made the best moves at the trade deadline. Phone lines burn by the second as friends bicker over who was the greatest of all time. Blogs and discussion forums explode to life when a blockbuster trade is made or a record is set. From the bar in Goose Bay to the snack line at GM Place in Vancouver, the fires of sports debate rage endlessly.

While this book isn't designed to settle bets, or to offer opinions on the greatest athletes in a given sport, it does engage Canadian sports fans in the ultimate debate: What are the greatest moments in Canadian sports history?

This book is, first and foremost, a thorough collection of the most celebrated events the country has ever seen. It will provide Canadians with a rare opportunity to see recent heroes like Cindy Klassen share the spotlight with classic Canadian icons like Maurice Richard. Also included are fresh new perspectives from the athletes themselves, as well as those whose lives were touched by the performances they witnessed. The book is a tapestry of dozens of sports, featuring athletes ranging from teenagers to 50-somethings. Every chapter tells a different, yet engaging, story.

But there's an added hook: the achievements are ranked.

With the help of a panel of Canadian sports personalities—including renowned sports broadcaster Chris Cuthbert, national columnist Stephen Brunt, and reporters from TSN, The Score, the *Toronto Sun*, and The Canadian Press—Canada's top 100 sports newsmakers have been forged into place, from number 100 all the way to number 1. Where does Steve Bauer's performance in the 1988 Tour de France rank all-time? Whose Olympic performance was considered more impressive: Gaetan Boucher's or Simon Whitfield's? Did Mike Weir's Masters top Steve Nash's back-to-back NBA Most Valuable Player nods?

The list is sure to ignite debates around the country. Hockey fans will undoubtedly wonder why more NHL moments didn't make the grade. Baseball aficionados will seethe at the sight of so many winter sports moments. Fans of fringe sports will throw up their hands at the predominance of pro sports moments. A precious few will be satisfied with the list in its entirety, and many will wonder if the panel knows anything about sports at all.

And frankly, that's just the way we want it.

Although there won't be much consensus on the rankings themselves, all readers can agree that the book provides a rare opportunity to soak in the most significant events in the history of Canadian sports all at once. Relive the memories of Wayne Gretzky's unprecedented 215-point season. Discover how a helping hand from an unlikely source guided Vic Emery to Canada's first Olympic medal in bobsledding. Learn about the spirit and courageousness of the late Terry Fox from none other than Rick Hansen.

One hundred chapters, 100 moments, and 100 reasons to take pride in the Maple Leaf. With more than 20 sports included, along with dazzling photos and dozens of up-to-date recollections from athletes, coaches, and media personalities, the book gives sports fans the most comprehensive look at their favourite Canadian sports memories.

And so, let the debate begin.

The Canadian Press/Frank Gunn

PAUL TRACY, KING OF CART (2003)

NOT EVEN PAUL TRACY could have predicted this.

The native of West Hill, Ont., signed with Player's/Forsythe Racing for the 2003 CART season, the auto-racing circuit's most sought-after free agent joining a team loaded with Canadian drivers. Following two disappointing campaigns with Team KOOL Green, Tracy was desperate to return to the form that saw him earn third-place finishes in both the 1993 and 1994 overall standings.

The Canadian Press/Paul Chiasson

He responded by putting together a season for the ages, earning his first series championship and cementing his place as one of the greatest open-wheel drivers in North America.

Tracy reeled off consecutive wins in Florida, Mexico, and California to become the first CART driver to open a season with three straight victories. He was headed for a fourth triumph after capturing the pole at the London Champ Car Trophy, but a faulty gearbox ended Tracy's race after 118 laps.

After twelfth-place finishes in Germany and Milwaukee, the 35-year-old lost his lead in the overall drivers' standings. The fiery Tracy responded with vigour, posting five consecutive podium finishes capped by wins in Toronto and Vancouver. Those victories made him the first homegrown driver to win a CART race in Canada.

Tracy picked up his sixth win in Ohio, equalling his entire victory total in five seasons with KOOL Green. A

seventh victory in Mexico City in October, combined with a late-season collapse by Bruno Junqueira, left Tracy in position to clinch the title in Australia.

He did just that after Junqueira crashed out of the race with 10 laps remaining.

"[My crew] said 'You are the champion.' I broke down for 20 or 30 seconds and started to cry inside the helmet," Tracy said after his victory. "Then they said 'OK, we got to get it together. We still need to finish this race and get points and really solidify it and make sure it's for real'" (The Canadian Press, October 26, 2003).

As a bonus, Tracy led Canada to the Nation's Cup title, giving the "Thrill from West Hill" a double that was equal parts rare and unexpected.

The Canadian Press/Richard Lam

MIKE VANDERJAGT GOES FIELD-GOAL CRAZY (2003)

IT'S A SHAME THAT NFL kicking star Mike Vanderjagt will likely be remembered most for his contributions away from the field.

Vanderjagt was an ornery fellow, ripping opposing NFL teams and even insulting his own head coach and quarterback in a famed television tirade. But the Oakville, Ont., native could also boot the football, putting together a solid career capped by the greatest kicking season in NFL history.

Vanderjagt, who began his football career in Toronto and returned to the Argos in 2008, arrived with the Indianapolis Colts in 1998 and was an immediate success. In his second full season, Vanderjagt led the NFL in scoring, making 34 of 38 field goals.

Canadian Press football reporter Dan Ralph believes Vanderjagt's tenure in the CFL served him well in the U.S.

"Kicking in the CFL had a major impact on his NFL career," said Ralph. "There are some really tough places to kick in Canada.

"Take the way the wind swirls in Winnipeg, for example. If you can kick there, you can kick anywhere."

Two more solid years followed before Vanderjagt hit the wall, missing eight field-goal attempts in one season. Following a 41–0 playoff loss to the New York Jets, Vanderjagt berated Colts head coach Tony Dungy and quarterback Peyton Manning in an interview on all-sports network The Score. With a terrible season on the field made worse by his public spat with Dungy and Manning, Vanderjagt's star had lost its lustre.

Vanderjagt's fortunes changed just as quickly, if only for one more star-studded season. He began 2003 with a flourish, making 10 field goals in his first three games, five of which came from at least 40 yards out. By season's end, Vanderjagt was a perfect 37-for-37, giving him the longest streak of successful attempts (42) in league history.

Vanderjagt's numbers dipped from there, and he left the league in 2006 after making just 13 of 18 field goals for the Dallas Cowboys. It was a strangely subdued exit for a man who had generated plenty of hype during his nine seasons in the NFL—both with his foot and with his mouth.

The Canadian Press/Tom Hanson

NESTOR AND LAREAU GOLDEN IN SYDNEY (2000)

IT WAS THE GOLD MEDAL no Canadian saw coming—except, perhaps, for the two men who actually won.

Canada's track record at the Olympic Summer Games isn't that strong, and the country isn't known for producing world-class tennis players. Fans were simply hoping for a strong result from Toronto's Daniel Nestor and Boucherville, Que., native Sebastien Lareau, perhaps culminating in a podium finish.

What they ended up with was a stunning gold medal, thanks to one of the most sensational performances in the history of Canadian tennis.

"It's always been a dream, ever since I was young and watching Olympics on TV," Lareau said following the victory. "I always wanted to be a part of that. Playing with Daniel, I knew we'd have a good shot of getting a medal" (The Canadian Press, September 27, 2000).

Nestor and Lareau dominated from the outset, steamrolling to a first-round win over the Brazilian duo Gustavo Kuerten and Jaime Oncins. The two followed with a straight-sets win over a Venezuelan tandem before trouncing Tommy Haas and David Prinosil of Germany in the quarter-final.

Nestor and Lareau were even more dangerous in the semifinal, blitzing David Adams and John-Laffnie De Jager of South Africa 6–1, 6–2, to set up a gold-medal showdown with the top-seeded crowd favourites Todd Woodbridge and Mark Woodforde. Facing the most successful team in doubles history in front of 10,000 boisterous fans at New South Wales Tennis Centre, a Canadian victory seemed improbable.

Two and a half hours later, the unlikely became reality.

A first-set defeat was the only blemish on the Canadians' run to gold, as Nestor and Lareau stormed back to win the next three sets in a wildly entertaining match. Both men declared the victory one of the highlights of their careers, and the duo was later named team of the year in voting by The Canadian Press and Broadcast News.

It was an unexpected honour for a team that provided Canada with an unexpected gold medal, but one the country was more than happy to embrace.

The Canadian Press/Ryan Remiorz

The Canadian Press/Frank Gunn

DAMON ALLEN BECOMES CFL PASS KING (2000)

The Canadian Press/Jonathan Hayward

DAMON ALLEN'S CFL career will be defined by two things: gaudy numbers, and the quiet nature with which he generated them.

On October 28, 2000, the legendary quarterback broke the silence by shattering one of the league's most sacred records. Allen's 45-yard touchdown pass to B.C. Lions teammate Alfred Jackson moved him past Ron Lancaster and into sole possession of first place on the CFL's all-time passing yards list. Allen would eventually rack up more than 20,000 additional passing yards to become the most prolific passer in pro football history.

Having his name listed alongside NFL legends Warren Moon, Dan Marino, and Brett Favre will always mean something special to Allen. But it was the Canadian record that immediately vaulted him up the short list of greatest quarterbacks in CFL history, and helped him shed the label as an erratic, mistake-prone passer.

"Inconsistency doesn't go with the numbers that I've done," Allen said after breaking the record. "It's always baffled me throughout my career. They've always said I've been inconsistent.

"You [can't] be inconsistent when you do the things I've done in this league. It doesn't weigh out" (The Canadian Press, October 29, 2000).

Needing 4,641 yards to pass Lancaster, Allen opened the 2000 season with a 394-yard performance in a 33–26 win over Hamilton. Six weeks later, he became the all-time completions leader with No. 3,384 in a 36–26 win over Toronto.

Heading into a late-October rematch with the Tiger-Cats, Allen needed just 175 yards to break the record. He reached the mark early in the second quarter, as Lancaster—then the Ticats head coach—looked on. Allen and Lancaster hugged at mid-field while the Lions unfurled a banner honouring the occasion.

In typical Allen fashion, the veteran was more pleased with the final game result: a 28–22 win that vaulted the Lions into the playoffs, where they would run the table on the way to their fourth Grey Cup championship.

The Canadian Press/Frank Gunn

MARC GAGNON'S OLYMPIC GOLD RUSH (2002)

MARC GAGNON replaced the monkey on his back with plenty of hardware around his neck.

The Chicoutimi, Que., native orchestrated an incredible performance at the 2002 Olympics, winning gold in both the men's 500-metre short-track speedskating event and as part of the 5,000-metre relay team. He added a bronze in the 1,500-metre event at Salt Lake City to end his Olympic career with a total of five medals, making him one of Canada's most decorated athletes.

Gagnon entered the 2002 Games with four world championships and two Olympic medals—a bronze in Lillehammer in 1994, and relay gold at the 1998 Games in Nagano. But he couldn't forget the disappointments he suffered two other times in Japan. Gagnon was disqualified from the 1,000 for impeding another skater; four days later, he slipped and fell during the 500, settling for fourth.

Despite finishing the Games with gold in the relay, Gagnon was haunted by his solo failures.

"I was disappointed enough to believe that I was done with speed skating," Gagnon admitted. "I actually took a year off, and that was supposed to be my retirement at the time. I figured it was time to go on with my life."

Gagnon returned to the sport, and eventually recaptured the form that made him one of the most feared skaters in the world. Armed with fresh legs and an outlook to match, he returned to the Olympics ready to capture the individual gold medal he was denied in Nagano.

After opening with a disappointing disqualification in the 1,000-metre race, Gagnon bounced back quickly, finishing third in the 1,500-metre event. His first solo medal now around his neck, a confident Gagnon topped the field in the 500, edging out teammate Jonathan Guilmette and U.S. skater Rusty Smith in the final.

A second gold in the relay later that day capped Gagnon's remarkable comeback, and gave him one final, satisfying chance to stand for his national anthem.

"There's no greater feeling when you're up there than seeing the Canadian flag," said Gagnon. "I was so proud of having done it for my country."

95

The Canadian Press/COC/Andre Forget

ADAM VAN KOEVERDEN, KING OF THE SEA (2004)

ADAM VAN KOEVERDEN entered the 2004 canoe and kayak season without a gold medal to his credit in his first three seasons as a senior.

By the time the year was over, van Koeverden had captured the unlikeliest championship of all—a gold medal in the 500-metre discipline at the Olympic Summer Games in Athens, a win that put him in exclusive company and earned him a place alongside Wayne Gretzky, Jacques Villeneuve, and Nancy Greene in Canadian sports annals.

Van Koeverden was expected to have a breakout season in 2004 after finishing second at the 2003 world championships in Gainesville, Fla. With Athens looming, the Oakville, Ont., native hit his stride, securing Olympic berths in both the 500- and 1,000-metre kayak events. At the final tune-up ahead of the Games, van Koeverden was nearly flawless in capturing two gold medals.

His next would come the following month, galvanizing his place as one of Canada's greatest open-water competitors. Having captured a bronze medal in the 1,000-metre event one day earlier, van Koeverden entered the 500-metre final with hopes of once again reaching the podium, even though the 500 was the weaker of his disciplines.

The Canadian Press/COC/Mike Ridewood

The Canadian Press/COC/Andre Forget

That didn't show in the final, as van Koeverden crossed the line in one minute, 37.919 seconds, edging out runner-up Nathan Baggaley of Australia.

"Once I looked to my left and right and realized there was nobody there, I threw my arm in the air and screamed," said van Koeverden. "The first thought in my head was, 'I'm an Olympic champion.' It was very emotional."

The multi-medal performance earned van Koeverden flag-bearer duties for the closing ceremony, and he went on to capture the 2004 Lou Marsh Award as Canada's top athlete, an incredible honour for a kayaker in a country dominated by winter sports.

"I look at the names of some of the athletes that have won that award, and I kind of feel outplayed a little bit," van Koeverden admitted. "Maybe a lot of other people feel that I am, too. I hope they don't."

The Canadian Press/Chuck Stoody

RANDY FERBEY WINS FOURTH WORLD TITLE (2005)

WITH THE GLUT OF world-class men's curling teams in Canada, the national playdowns often end up being more of a challenge than the actual world championship.

But you won't get Randy Ferbey to subscribe to that belief—not after the roller-coaster his Edmonton foursome faced at the 2005 worlds in Victoria, where Ferbey earned his fourth world title.

The Canadian Press/Chuck Stoody

Ferbey, lead Marcel Rocque, second Scott Pfeifer, and third Dave Nedohin opened the worlds with a 10–5 clunker to Germany. Victories over New Zealand and Sweden eased Canadians' minds, but an 8–7 loss to the U.S. left Canada at 2–2. After beating Finland and Denmark, Ferbey suffered a 5–4 heartbreaker to Norway that put him at three losses for the tournament. One more defeat, and his rink would be history.

"There's always extra pressure whenever you're not playing well at home," said Nedohin. "But we knew we just had to keep doing what got us there in the first place."

Canada followed with comfortable victories against minnows Italy and Switzerland before beating Scotland 8–4 and edging Australia 8–7 in the round-robin finale to cram into a six-way tie for top spot.

After the playoff picture was sorted out, Ferbey found himself in a tiebreaker against Finland, won 9–5 by the Canadians. A steal of one in the tenth end gave Ferbey a 7–6 win over Norway in the quarter-finals, and he continued his heroics in the semifinals, taking three with the hammer in the tenth end of an 8–6 triumph over Germany.

Canada saved its most dominant performance for the final. Trailing 2–1 against Scotland, Ferbey's rink scored five in the third end, a record for a world championship match. Ferbey put up another five in the seventh, and the title was his one end later with the score 11–4.

It took eight straight wins to get there, but the Ferbey foursome was back on top of the curling world.

"That may have been our most rewarding victory," Nedohin said. "Combined with winning the Brier in Edmonton, that was probably the greatest stretch of my career."

The Canadian Press/Chuck Stoody

The Canadian Press/Joe Bryksa

LUI SAVES THE DAY FOR B.C. (1994)

IN A GAME THAT WOULD change the CFL forever, it was a diminutive kicker from Vancouver who booted his way into Canadian sports immortality.

Lui Passaglia's 38-yard field goal as time expired gave the B.C. Lions an emotional 26–23 victory over the Baltimore CFLers in the first Grey Cup ever contested between Canada and the United States. Passaglia's line-drive kick kept the hallowed trophy from heading south for the first time in its 82-year existence.

"To be in that situation where you get to play the game you love and do it at home in front of your fans, and the rest of Canada, and being Grey Cup champions, it's incredible," said Passaglia.

"And best of all, you get to say you kept the Grey Cup in Canada."

Enjoying a remarkable inaugural season, the CFLers trounced the Toronto Argonauts 34–15 in the East semifinal before sneaking past Winnipeg 14–12 to advance to the Grey Cup. The Lions reached the title game by upset-ting Calgary 37–36 in a legendary West final, setting the stage for an historic Canada–U.S. showdown.

Passaglia put B.C. out in front 3–0 with a 47-yarder early in the game. Baltimore replied with a pair of touchdowns in the second quarter, and enjoyed a 17–10 advantage at the half. The Lions stormed back in the third quarter on a one-yard TD run from quarterback Danny McManus and Passaglia's 42-yard field goal.

Tied 23–23 late in the fourth quarter, Passaglia had a chance to put the Lions ahead with a 37-yarder with 1:02 left. He missed, sending a collective groan through the crowd of 55,097 at B.C. Place.

The Lions responded by stopping the CFLers on their next drive, getting the ball back in excellent field position. Moments later, Passaglia was called upon to make the most important kick of his life. With no time left on the clock, Passaglia took three steps and booted a low, straight kick between the uprights, propelling the Lions to one of the most emotionally charged Grey Cup titles in history.

The Canadian Press/Chuck Stoody

JUNIORS BACK ON TOP OF THE HOCKEY WORLD (2005)

LITTLE GOOD CAME OF the lockout that crippled the National Hockey League for 310 days and resulted in the cancellation of the entire 2004–2005 season.

But Canada's world junior team used the work stoppage to its advantage, ending the country's seven-year gold-medal drought in Grand Forks, N.D., by putting together a truly dominant performance, capped by a 6–1 win over Russia in a one-sided final.

After losing a heartbreaker to Russia a year earlier, Hockey Canada assembled an armada of talent for the 2005 event. Future NHLers to wear the red and white that year included Pittsburgh Penguins superstar Sidney Crosby, Boston Bruins sniper Patrice Bergeron, and Calgary Flames bruiser Dion Phaneuf.

"We had experience, we had the talent, but we still felt like we had to prove ourselves," said Phaneuf. "There was a lot of leftover disappointment from the year before. We definitely had to have a big tournament."

The Canadians showed little mercy in preliminary action, posting a 4–0 record while outscoring their opponents 32–5. The team's first real test came in the semifinal, where they faced the talented Czechs. Nigel Dawes scored the game winner, Jeff Carter and Bergeron also had goals, and the defence frustrated the Czechs in Canada's 3–1 win.

The victory set up a gold-medal showdown with Russia for the third time in four years. The Russians, led by young guns Evgeni Malkin and Alexander Ovechkin, had beaten Canada in the previous two finals.

Ryan Getzlaf opened the scoring 51 seconds into the game, and Canada rode the early momentum to a 2–1 lead after 20 minutes. The second period saw the Canadians blast the Russians for four unanswered goals in a 14-minute span that rendered the third period meaningless, giving Canada its first title since 1997. The 6–1 result was the most lopsided championship score in tournament history.

"We had a clear game plan, and we stuck with it," said Phaneuf. "We were a hard-working team with plenty of grit, but we had the skill to back it up.

"We knew what we had to do to win, and we executed."

FLAMES BEAT HABS IN ALL-CANADIAN CUP (1989)

THE ODDS AGAINST AN all-Canadian Stanley Cup final are long. With just six Canadian-based franchises in a 30-team league, the nation's fans are thrilled when even one team reaches the best-of-seven championship.

It wasn't always that way—just ask fans in Calgary and Montreal. In 1989, the Canadiens and Flames staged an entertaining six-game series that saw the Flames capture their first Stanley Cup, atoning for their loss to Montreal in the 1986 final.

The Canadiens cruised to the 1989 final, sweeping Hartford before wiping out Boston in five games and knocking off Philadelphia in six. Then–rookie forward Mike Keane says the strong playoff performance left the Canadiens brimming with confidence entering the final.

"We felt great about our chances," said Keane. "We had built a well-balanced team—great scoring, great defence, and superb goaltending."

Calgary needed seven games to upend Vancouver in a classic first-round series. From there, the Flames tore through Los Angeles and Chicago, losing just one game in the two series combined.

After the Habs and Flames split the first two games in Calgary, Ryan Walter's double-overtime goal in Game 3 gave Montreal a 2–1 series lead. The Flames responded with a 4–2 victory in Game 4 before delighting the Saddledome crowd in Game 5 with a 3–2 win.

Two nights later, Lanny McDonald provided the Flames with the biggest goal in franchise history. With the teams tied 1–1 in Game 6, McDonald had the go-ahead goal in the second period for his first score of the post-season, and the final goal of his 16-year career. Calgary won 4–2, becoming the first road team to win the Stanley Cup in Montreal's home building.

To this day, the 1989 final remains the last all-Canadian Stanley Cup matchup. And with 80 percent of NHL franchises based in the U.S., it could be a while before it happens again.

"Because there were two Canadian teams involved, it was very exciting for the country," said Keane. "But it was nowhere near what it would be like if it happened now."

The Canadian Press/COC

CANADA CAPTURES FOUR-MAN BOBSLED GOLD (1964)

WHEN VIC EMERY RECEIVED his gold medal at the 1964 Winter Olympics in Innsbruck, Austria, he must have been tempted to invite Eugenio Monti to join him on the podium.

Were it not for Monti's remarkable gesture, Emery's four-man bobsled crew would not have been able to pull off one of the greatest upsets in the history of the sport.

Emery, his brother John, Doug Anakin, and Peter Kirby were the ultimate underdogs of bobsled. Having to rely largely on dry-land runs in Montreal, the team languished behind the rest of the world. Without government funding, the men paid their own way to events while competing in a dilapidated sled.

The Canadian Press/COC

Despite their struggles, they found a way to make it to Innsbruck, forming Canada's first-ever Olympic bobsled team. What happened next defied the odds: the Canadian sled rocketed down the course in a record time of one minute, 2.99 seconds, putting the unheralded Canucks nearly a half-second ahead of their closest competitors.

The blistering run came at a steep cost. Emery's sled had a seized axle, and if it couldn't be fixed in time for their second run, the team would be disqualified. Enter

Monti, the well-respected Italian champion. Recognizing the Canadians' dilemma, Monti and his mechanics helped repair the sled just minutes before Emery's second run.

The Canadian Press/COC

Canada took full advantage of the unexpected gift, posting impressive times in the second and third runs to expand its lead over runner-up Austria to nine-tenths of a second. Not wishing to sit back and relax, Emery's team finished the competition with the fastest fourth-run time, locking up a 1.02-second victory and securing one of the most unlikely gold medals in Olympic history. Austria placed second, while Monti's foursome captured bronze.

It would be several more years before Canada would begin to embrace bobsled the way other world powers did. While that may not have been what Emery had in mind, it only makes his victory in 1964—and the story that goes with it—that much more remarkable.

89

BECKIE SCOTT FINALLY GETS HER GOLD (2004)

BECKIE SCOTT MAY BE the only athlete in Olympic history to win three medals for the same event. In the end, she kept the best one.

The Vermilion, Alta., native was awarded a gold medal more than two years after the race actually happened. The 2004 presentation in Vancouver ended a bizarre saga in which two Russian skiers were stripped of their medals after testing positive for the same banned substance.

"Even though it took so long, I can still say I am an Olympic champion," Scott said. "I won a race at the Olympics and reached the pinnacle of my career. It's a pretty remarkable thing for an athlete to say."

The 5-kilometre pursuit was highlighted by a spirited duel between Russian teammates Olga Danilova and Larissa Lazutina. Danilova went on to win by nearly seven seconds over Lazutina, while Scott rallied over the last few metres and lunged to the line one-tenth of a second ahead of Katerina Neumannova of the Czech Republic.

Not long after receiving her medal, things became even more interesting for Scott.

Both Danilova and Lazutina tested positive for the banned substance darbepoetin, which helps increase the blood's oxygen-carrying capacity. The Russians were allowed to keep their medals from the 5-kilometre event because the positive tests occurred well after the race had been run.

The Canadian Olympic Committee claimed Lazutina had failed a pair of tests prior to the Olympics. The International Olympic Committee ruled in Canada's favour, and Lazutina was stripped of both medals she had won at Salt Lake City. On October 21, 2003, Scott was officially awarded the silver medal.

Less than two months later, the Court of Arbitration for Sport ruled that Danilova be stripped of her Olympic medals as well. The following June, Scott received her long-awaited gold medal at the Vancouver Art Gallery.

"I felt tremendous relief that everything had worked out, in a totally weird, roundabout way," recalled Scott.

"There was also a sense of vindication. We came out on the good side. Justice was done."

The Canadian Press/Moe Doiron

CLEMENS COPS BACK-TO-BACK CYS (1997–1998)

THERE WASN'T MUCH TO cheer about in Toronto in the years after the Blue Jays won back-to-back World Series titles in 1992 and 1993.

Roger Clemens changed all that in a hurry. Though Clemens's stay in Canada was a brief one, and had little impact on the team's won-lost record, it provided fans with a glimpse at two of the greatest single-season pitching performances in the history of the game.

Clemens signed for big bucks—U.S. $24.75 million over three years—to help the Jays return to respectability following consecutive 88-loss seasons. Clemens also looked to resurrect his career after two subpar years with the Boston Red Sox.

"When he came here, nobody really knew what to expect," said Canadian Press baseball writer Shi Davidi. "But he came to Toronto as motivated as ever. He really wanted to show people how good he was."

Clemens was an instant hit, tossing a complete-game six-hitter for the win in his Toronto debut. The 34-year-old would go on to win his first 11 decisions as a Blue Jay and finished the year 21–7 with a 2.05 ERA and a career-high 292 strikeouts, earning his fourth Cy Young.

Unfortunately, the Jays failed to take advantage, finishing 76–86—22 games behind the division-winning Baltimore Orioles.

Clemens got off to a rough start in 1998, sitting at 5–6 after a loss to Cleveland in late May. "Rocket Roger" wouldn't lose another game all season, rifling off a franchise-record 15 victories over his final 22 starts. He led the league in wins (20), strikeouts (271), and ERA (2.65) for the second straight season, capturing yet another Cy Young.

While the Jays improved to 88 wins, they were no match for the New York Yankees, who put up a staggering 114 victories. That winter, Clemens requested a trade out of Toronto, no longer satisfied with treading water

on a non-playoff team. The Jays grudgingly obliged, and Clemens was shipped to the Bronx, leaving Toronto with plenty of personal accomplishments, but falling well short in his quest to return the Jays to playoff glory.

The Canadian Press/Frank Gunn

The Canadian Press/COC

SCHMIRLER WINS THIRD WORLD TITLE (1997)

WHEN SANDRA SCHMIRLER LED her Saskatchewan-based rink to victory at the 1997 Scott Tournament of Hearts, she became just the third woman in Canadian history to win three national championships.

A few months later, Schmirler entered even more rarefied air. Schmirler, Jan Betker, Joan McCusker, and Marcia Gudereit became the first Canadian women's team to win three world championships, a record that still has not been equalled.

"We were very much aware that we were setting a record," said McCusker. "We were really, really proud of that accomplishment.

"I can't even begin to tell you how competitive we are. We used to joke about how we didn't like to lose anything, so this win meant a lot to each of us."

After going 11–2 at the Scott, the talented quartet was tested right away at the worlds in Berne, Switzerland, facing Norwegian curling legend Dordi Nordby in the round-robin opener. Canada won 5–3 in a cautiously played game, following that up with victories over the United States, Japan, Switzerland, and Scotland.

Riding high at 5–0, Schmirler suffered her only slip of the round-robin, an 8–5 defeat to Germany. That loss seemed to invigorate the Schmirler rink, which concluded the round-robin with lopsided victories over Finland, Sweden, and Denmark.

"When you're playing well, sometimes you get complacent," said McCusker. "We understood that sometimes a loss is a good thing. It doesn't feel good to lose, but we used it as a way to get back on track."

Canada beat Denmark 5–2 in one semifinal, while Norway trounced Japan 12–5 in the other, setting up a rematch of the opening game of the tournament.

The teams played to a 1–1 tie through four ends before Schmirler took control with a five-point fifth end. Nordby's second-half rally fell short, and the Canadians held on for an 8–4 victory.

For good measure, Schmirler would later lead her rink to a berth in the 1998 Olympics later in the year. That accomplishment, combined with her national and world titles, make Schmirler's 1997 campaign one of the greatest 12-month stretches in Canadian curling history.

The Canadian Press/COC

The Associated Press/Dawn Villella

GORDIE HOWE HITS THE ICE AT AGE 51 (1980)

GORDIE HOWE WAS ALWAYS EAGER to give his fans a thrill, even when he was old enough to be their grandfather.

In 1980, the NHL legend did the unthinkable, suiting up for the Hartford Whalers as a 51-year-old. Howe finished with a respectable 41 points while playing all 80 regular-season games and adding three more appearances in the post-season.

Howe was one of the NHL's first superstars, recording 14 30-goal seasons during his two-decade career with the Detroit Red Wings. But his playing days ended after the 1970–1971 season, as arthritic wrists hampered his ability to compete at a high level.

"The fun had left the game," Howe said. "I was hurting. Hockey had become labour, and that's when I knew it was time to move on."

The Associated Press

He left the NHL holding every major scoring record, and his induction into the Hockey Hall of Fame in 1972 seemed a fitting end to Howe's career.

A year later, Howe served in the Red Wings' front office. The role didn't suit Howe, and after sons Mark and Marty were drafted by the Houston Aeros of the World Hockey Association, Gordie considered joining them.

"The love of the game had returned," Howe said, "and it had always been a dream of mine to play with my boys. I only hoped I wasn't going to look like an old man out there."

The Canadian Press/Doug Ball

Howe's return couldn't have gone any better—he scored 21 seconds into his first game, with Mark drawing an assist. Gordie went on to win the MVP award with 100 points, and the Aeros captured the championship.

Howe spent three more seasons with the Aeros and two with the New England Whalers before the WHA merged with the NHL, and the Whalers franchise moved to Hartford. Howe returned to the NHL after an eight-year absence, and was selected to his record twenty-third all-star game—at Joe Louis Arena in Detroit, no less.

There, tens of thousands of appreciative fans gave him two standing ovations, the ultimate tribute to hockey's ultimate elder statesman.

The Canadian Press/Ryan Remiorz

CANADIENS GO OT-HAPPY IN CUP WIN (1993)

A LITTLE EXTRA HOCKEY paid off in a big way for the 1992–1993 Montreal Canadiens.

Thanks to some timely goals and a few lucky bounces, the Canadiens put together an astounding playoff run that featured 10 straight overtime victories and culminated with their twenty-fourth Stanley Cup title. It also marked the last time a Canadian team has won the championship.

The Canadiens opened the playoffs with series wins over Quebec and Buffalo. Five of Montreal's eight victories came in extra time, including three straight OT wins over the Sabres by identical 4–3 scores.

Next up were the New York Islanders, who had knocked off the two-time defending champions from Pittsburgh. After the Canadiens earned a 4–1 win in Game 1, it was back to OT for Montreal—a 4–3, double-OT win in Game 2, followed by a 2–1 overtime triumph in Game 3.

Before they knew it, the Canadiens had become the NHL's version of the "Cardiac Kids."

"We weren't really thinking about it at the time," said Canadiens forward Mike Keane. "We'd be down a goal, and just work as hard as we could to get it to overtime. Once we got there, we were very confident."

A 4–1 loss in Game 4 brought the Habs' 11-game winning streak to an end, but Montreal quickly regrouped with a series-clinching 5–2 win in Game 5.

Montreal's quest for the Cup went through Los Angeles. The Kings opened with a 4–1 win before the overtime specialists struck again in record fashion. The Canadiens earned a 2–1 OT win in Game 2, then rode back-to-back overtime winners from John LeClair to take a stranglehold on the series.

Having deflated the Kings, Montreal cruised to a 4–1 win in Game 5 to clinch the Stanley Cup, one of their few victories that didn't require more than 60 minutes to finish. At that moment, the hours of extra hockey didn't seem so bad; after all, the players now had the entire summer to rest, recover, and savour the biggest victory of their professional careers.

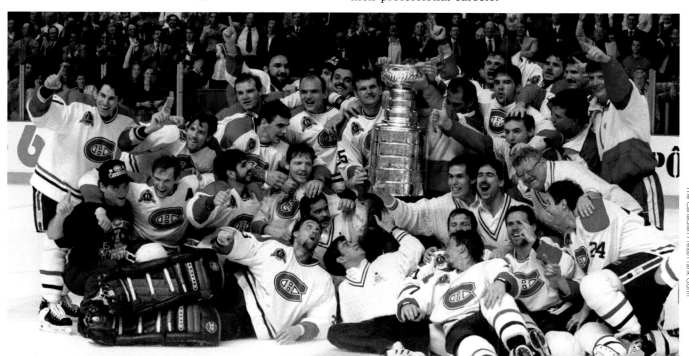

84

The Canadian Press/COC/T.Grant

BATTLE OF THE BRIANS (1988)

TO MOST CANADIANS, the only thing that could have enhanced the men's figure-skating event at the 1988 Olympics was a Brian Orser victory.

Orser settled for silver, but the result did little to tarnish what many consider to be one of the greatest competitions in the history of the sport. Orser and American rival Brian Boitano battled down to the end, matching flawless performances in a showdown Orser lost by the slimmest of margins.

The legendary duel made headlines around the world, and Orser was grateful to have been a part of it, despite the second-place finish.

"I was flattered that such a big deal was made about it," said Orser. "I know that in the long run, it was one of the best things for my career as a professional skater because I was one of the two Brians.

"It kind of evened things out at the end of the day."

The Boitano-Orser rivalry reached its apex at Calgary, with each man owning a world championship win over the other. The Brians split the first two portions of the Olympic competition, with Boitano capturing the compulsory figures and Orser winning the short program. Whoever skated a better long program would win gold.

Boitano skated first in the long program, wowing the crowd with a technically perfect skate. He earned 5.8s and 5.9s after landing eight triple jumps, though his so-so artistic marks left room for Orser to seize the win.

Orser landed only seven triple jumps, but was artistically superior to Boitano. Yet, despite earning a 6.0 from the Czechoslovakian judge, Orser placed first on just four of nine scorecards. Boitano won gold, Orser took home silver, and fans went home with memories of a truly incredible competition between two figure-skating giants.

"We both now realize how big it was in the history of our sport," said Orser. "At the time, it was just sort of fun. Now, we do a lot of reflecting back on the Battle of the Brians, and we just go 'Wow, we did that.'"

The Canadian Press/COC/ C. McNeil

The Canadian Press/COC/J Merrithew

STEVE BAUER'S TOUR DE FORCE (1988)

STEVE BAUER LOOKS awfully good in yellow.

The Fenwick, Ont., native had plenty of experience in 1988, wearing the leader's yellow jersey for five days at the Tour de France, cycling's most gruelling endurance event. Bauer finished fourth in the three-week marathon, the best-ever result by a Canadian and one of the most impressive individual achievements in the nation's history.

"It's at the top of my list," said Bauer. "It's without a doubt the best physical and mental performance I've ever had on a bike.

"I've done well in other races, but cumulatively that's a big one, to be able to put it all together for the Tour."

Fresh off a successful amateur career that included second-place finishes at the 1982 Commonwealth Games and 1984 Summer Olympics, Bauer focused on the sport's elite events, particularly the Tour de France. He placed tenth in 1985, twenty-third the following year, and plummeted to seventy-fourth in 1987.

Vowing to make amends, Bauer captured the opening stage in 1988. He became just the second Canadian to ever lead cycling's signature race, joining Alex Stieda, who led after the second day of competition in 1986.

Though Bauer relinquished the yellow jersey the next day, he would get it back a week later, and held on to it for three more days. Bauer went on to finish the 3,281-kilometre trek just 12 minutes, 15 seconds behind race winner Pedro Delgado of Spain.

Bauer went on to finish fifteenth in 1989 and led nine stages of the 1990 race en route to a twenty-seventh-place result. He participated in the Tour until 1995, and announced his retirement the following summer. Bauer's accomplishments against the world's best earned him induction into both the Canadian Olympic Hall of Fame and the Canadian Sports Hall of Fame in 2005.

Bauer says few experiences in his career compared with the thrill of slipping on the leader's yellow shirt.

"That's the one true trophy everybody aims for," said Bauer. "Winning any stage of the Tour de France, or holding the overall lead, is a really big deal."

The Canadian Press/COC/J Merrithew

The Associated Press/Charlie Riedel

CANADA'S CLASSIC UPSET OVER THE U.S. (2006)

NOBODY KNEW WHAT TO EXPECT when the best base-ball nations in the world gathered for the inaugural World Baseball Classic.

What resulted was an outstanding tournament, featuring plenty of spectacular fielding, clutch hitting, memorable pitching, and genuine tension. There was even an upset or two, the most stunning coming from a group of plucky Canadians playing the role of giant-killers against a powerhouse U.S. team.

The Associated Press/Charlie Riedel

"It was extremely exciting … probably a little too ex-citing for March baseball," joked Pittsburgh Pirates star Jason Bay. "You can't simulate that type of emotion. It was quite a fun time."

The Canadians squeaked past South Africa 11–8 in their first game, leaving many to wonder how they would handle a U.S. squad laden with all-stars, Cy Young Award winners, and future Hall of Famers. They would answer that question the very next day.

Canada seized an early lead on a Stubby Clapp triple and a Justin Morneau RBI groundout. The underdogs added one more run in the second, a three-spot in the third, two more in the fourth, and a single run in the fifth on an inside-the-park home run from Boston Red Sox farmhand Adam Stern. By the game's halfway point, Canada had an 8–0 lead.

Embarrassed by their performance, the Americans got angry, and nearly got even in the process, scoring six times in the bottom of the fifth to carve Canada's lead down to 8–6. That was as close as the U.S. would get, with minor-league pitcher Steve Green inducing Texas Rangers slugger Mark Teixeira to ground out to first for the final out.

Canada would be knocked out of the tournament with a 9–1 loss to Mexico the next day, but the defeat did nothing to diminish what the team had accomplished. Behind spectacular fielding, clutch hitting, memorable pitching—and some late-game tension—the Canadians had achieved one of the biggest upsets in baseball history.

"It was obviously huge for us," said Bay. "Beating them probably did more for baseball in Canada than if we had moved on."

The Associated Press/Charles Rex Arbogast

The Associated Press/Gene J. Puskar

JASON BAY NAMED NL ROOKIE OF THE YEAR (2004)

IT'S RARE FOR A BASEBALL PLAYER to end up on four major-league teams before he plays his first game in the big show.

It's even more unusual to see that player capture Rookie of the Year honours.

Jason Bay has done both, with the latter achievement placing Bay in exclusive company. He's the first Canadian to win rookie honours in major-league history—an accomplishment the Trail, B.C., native takes seriously, even if he didn't at first.

The Associated Press/Paul Connors

"Initially, I didn't really give much thought to it," Bay admitted. "After, when you sit back and think about it and you get time to reflect on it, it does mean a little bit more."

Bay kicked around several minor-league circuits at the start of his career while major-league teams swapped him around. Bay arrived with the Pittsburgh Pirates in August 2003 from San Diego, which had acquired him from the New York Mets, who had picked him up from the Montreal Expos. Bay enjoyed limited success as a late-season call-up, but he began 2004 on the shelf after undergoing left-shoulder surgery in the off-season.

He returned to the lineup May 7, and while the batting average was solid, the power numbers weren't. Then came June 12, when Bay had three hits and two RBIs in a 12–11 loss to the Oakland Athletics. That kick-started Bay's Rookie of the Year push, as the left fielder hit .382 with nine home runs and 30 RBIs over his next 20 games.

Bay maintained a .300 average until early September, finishing up at .282. He led all major-league rookies in home runs (26) and RBIs (82), beating out Khalil Greene of the San Diego Padres for National League Rookie-of-the-Year honours.

Not bad for a guy who spent the beginning of his career being passed around more than a baseball card.

"It definitely wasn't the ideal path," said Bay. "When you're writing your story, that's not usually how you write it. But I think it had a large part in the makeup of the player and the person that I am today."

The Associated Press/Pat Sullivan

80

The Associated Press/Keith Srakocic

SIDNEY'S SENSATIONAL SEASON (2007)

SIDNEY CROSBY MAY NOT break all of Wayne Gretzky's records, but the Cole Harbour, N.S., native has already shown that comparisons to "The Great One" are well founded.

The Canadian Press/Frank Gunn

Crosby lit up the NHL in the 2006–2007 season, following his 100-point rookie campaign with a season for the history books. The Pittsburgh Penguins phenom had 36 goals and 84 assists to become the youngest player to ever win a league scoring title, breaking a record Gretzky had held for a quarter-century.

Crosby had a simple reason for his 120-point explosion: "I just wanted to be better than I was before."

Crosby entered 2006–2007 with high hopes, and a fast start proved a sign of things to come. The Rookie of the Year runner-up had six points in his first three games and capped the month of October with his first career hat trick in an 8–2 pounding of state rival Philadelphia. He was even better in November, closing with five straight multi-point games.

Crosby followed with his strongest run of the season, fashioning a 10-game point streak that included a career-best six-point performance against the Flyers. By the time he skated in his first all-star game, Crosby had an eye-popping 72 points in 43 games.

Despite slowing down in the second half, Crosby won the scoring title by six points over San Jose forward Joe Thornton. Crosby took home the Art Ross Trophy as scoring champion, the Hart Trophy as league MVP, and the Lester B. Pearson Award as NHLPA Player of the Year. Only seven players have ever captured the Hart-Ross-Pearson trifecta—none as young as Crosby, who wouldn't turn 20 for another eight weeks.

Like Gretzky did often throughout his career, Crosby thanked his parents first and foremost.

"The sacrifices of my parents, the early mornings, the practices … I owe a lot of thanks to them," he said (The Canadian Press, June 15, 2007).

Crosby capped his year by winning the Lou Marsh Award, becoming the first hockey player to do so since Mario Lemieux in 1993. Eight years after watching "The Great One" skate his final shift, the NHL officially had its "Next One."

The Canadian Press/Jonathan Hayward

Imperial Oil-Turofsky/Hockey Hall of Fame

LEAFS RALLY TO BEAT WINGS (1942)

WHENEVER A TEAM falls behind 3–0 in a best-of-seven series, three professional sports teams are once again thrust into the spotlight.

The 1975 New York Islanders stormed back from three games down to stun the Pittsburgh Penguins in the second round of the NHL playoffs. Nearly 30 years later, the Boston Red Sox upended the rival New York Yankees in the American League Championship series after losing the first three games.

And then there's the 1942 Toronto Maple Leafs, the first team in North American pro sports to erase a 3–0 deficit—and the only one to do it in a championship series—ousting the Detroit Red Wings to win the Stanley Cup.

The Wings used a dump-and-chase strategy—relatively new to the NHL at the time—to gain the early edge on the Leafs, leaving Maple Leaf Gardens with victories of 3–2 and 4–2. The Wings easily handled the Leafs 5–2 in Game 3, leaving Toronto head coach Hap Day scrambling for solutions.

Toronto escaped Detroit with a 4–3 victory in Game 4 behind Nick Metz's goal with 7:15 left in regulation. Heading back to Toronto with some of their confidence restored, the Leafs found their groove in Game 5, trouncing the listless Wings 9–3 behind three goals and two assists from Don Metz.

Don shone again in Game 6, breaking a 0–0 deadlock in the opening minute of the second period. Leafs goaltender Turk Broda made the lead stand up, stopping everything thrown his way in Toronto's 3–0 win. The series was suddenly tied, with the seventh and deciding game taking place at the Gardens.

With a Canadian-record crowd of 16,218 packed into the arena, Detroit nursed a 1–0 lead after 40 minutes. Sweeney Schriner tied the game at 6:46, and Pete Langelle followed with the eventual Cup-winning goal just over three minutes later. Schriner's second of the game put things out of reach with less than four minutes remaining, and the Leafs held on for their second Stanley Cup, won on the strength of the most improbable comeback in NHL history.

Imperial Oil-Turofsky/Hockey Hall of Fame

The Associated Press/Doug Mills

ELVIS STOJKO GUTS OUT OLYMPIC SILVER (1998)

FIGURE SKATERS ARE RARELY lauded for their toughness, at least compared to their on-ice brethren from the hockey world.

But after battling a career-threatening injury to reach the podium at the 1998 Winter Olympics in Nagano, diminutive skater Elvis Stojko put even the most rugged NHLer to shame.

Stojko's injury troubles began well before the Olympics. He captured the Canadian championship in January despite suffering a torn abductor muscle and a pinched nerve in his groin. Making things worse was a nagging flu he picked up while training in Nagano. While Stojko's camp did everything in its power to keep the media from discovering the skater's weakened state, Stojko tried to find a way to work through it all.

"My confidence level was still quite good," said Stojko. "I'd skated with injuries before. It was just a pull, and I felt I could deal with it.

"I was very aware of what it took to keep it from getting worse."

The Canadian skated an efficient short program that placed him second behind Ilya Kulik of Russia. But Stojko was suffering: he could barely get around the next day, which made practice excruciatingly painful.

After hitting his opening triple lutz in the long program, he downgraded his quad-triple combination into a triple-triple, focusing solely on skating a clean program. He went on to land all eight triples he attempted, running purely on adrenalin.

His stunning third-place result in the free skate put him second overall. Barely able to walk, Stojko hobbled to the podium in his running shoes, each step shooting waves of pain through his groin.

"After a couple of days, the pain kicked in even worse," Stojko admitted. "The adrenalin was gone. But it was then that I realized, 'Wow, I got a silver out of it.'"

Stojko became emotional once he realized the impact his performance had on fans around the world, especially children, who bombarded him with letters wishing him well. But don't let the tears fool you. As Stojko proved in Nagano, he's as tough as they come.

BRIAN ORSER: ON TOP OF THE WORLD (1987)

BEING THE BEST FIGURE SKATER in the country was only giving Brian Orser so much satisfaction.

He wanted to be the best in the world and, in 1987, the native of Orillia, Ont., finally got his wish, beating rival Brian Boitano on his home turf in the process. The victory not only gave Canada its first men's world champion in 24 years, it also served as the precursor to the "Battle of the Brians" at the 1988 Winter Olympics in Calgary, widely considered one of the greatest battles in figure-skating history.

"I really did feel that I was one of the best skaters in the world, if not the best," said Orser. "I needed to be and I wanted to be a front-runner in this sport.

"It felt like it fit being the best in the world, and I felt like I could handle that position."

Orser's confidence heading into Cincinnati was at an all-time high following a win over Boitano at Skate Canada. His unflappable demeanour served him well on U.S. soil, where Boitano was clearly the sentimental choice. Orser's short program was nearly flawless, and vaulted him to the top of the standings after day one.

Being in front seemed to put Orser at ease, and he came out on March 12, 1987, with gold on his mind. Orser chose to attempt two triple Axels rather than a single quad, and the result was another clean performance, a victory in the long program, and his first world championship at age 25.

Orser turned pro shortly after winning silver at the 1988 Olympics in Calgary, finishing his amateur career with one of the most impressive resumés in Canadian figure-skating history. And thanks to a pair of brilliant performances in Cincinnati in 1987, that resumé includes a world championship.

"That was a huge relief for me because I couldn't imagine going through the rest of my skating life without a world title," said Orser. "It's one of those things that nobody can take away."

76

BRAD GUSHUE'S RINK GOLDEN IN TURIN (2006)

WHEN BRAD GUSHUE REALIZED his foursome might not be good enough to win the Olympic trials, he went to a friend for help.

That "friend" turned out to be curling legend Russ Howard, so it surprised few that Gushue not only won the trials, but went on to capture an historic gold medal.

Gushue, lead Jamie Korab, second Mike Adam, and third Mark Nichols had originally brought Howard in as a fifth man, eager to draw from the experience of a two-time Brier and world champion. Yet, just a month before the trials, Gushue's situation changed.

"Things weren't going so smoothly for us at the start of the season," said Gushue. "We said, 'Why should we have one of the greatest players in the history of the game just sitting on the bench?' So we put him in."

After advancing to the Olympics, Gushue's rink opened the Games by winning four of its first five matches. Then, disaster struck in the form of back-to-back losses to Finland and Italy. Sitting at 4–3, Gushue knew he couldn't lose another game.

"We were pretty much panicking then," said Gushue. "Those were two teams we were expecting to beat. We knew we would have our hands full just getting into the playoffs."

Canada slipped into the final four with victories in its final two round-robin games. Taking on the U.S. in the semifinal, Gushue broke open a 6–5 game with five in the ninth end to earn a trip to the final.

Gushue battled Finland in the gold-medal match, where the Canadians found themselves in another tightly contested game. Again, Gushue relied on the big end, blasting the Finns with a six-pointer in the sixth on the way to a 10–4 rout.

With assistance from Howard, Gushue became Canada's first Olympic men's champion, an achievement the St. John's, Nfld., native says he'll cherish forever.

"It was one of the greatest experiences of my life," Gushue said. "Standing on that podium, listening to 'O Canada' … it still gives me chills every time I think about it."

The Canadian Press/Edmonton Sun/Christine Vanzella

NBA WELCOMES VANCOUVER, TORONTO (1993–1994)

WHEN THE NBA DECIDED to expand into Canada in the early 1990s, it had no idea how successful—or disastrous—the move would be.

It turned out to be both.

The Vancouver Grizzlies and Toronto Raptors joined the league in tandem in 1995, giving Canadian hoops fans two rooting interests to choose from. And while things didn't pan out in B.C., the Raptors became a stable franchise that won the hearts of basketball aficionados from across the country.

The birth of the Raptors can be traced back to Toronto businessman John Bitove, who led a consortium interested in bringing NBA basketball to the city. Knowing the SkyDome would be unsuitable as a permanent venue, Bitove's group presented the NBA with its plan for a new downtown arena. Two months later, the league's board of directors approved Toronto's bid.

Arthur Griffiths's group went to the expansion committee itself during all-star weekend in February 1994. There, the Vancouver businessman presented his plan for an arena that would house both the Canucks and the yet-to-be-awarded NBA team in time for the 1995–1996 season. The board of governors gave Griffiths the thumbs-up, and Canada suddenly had a pair of NBA franchises.

"This was a very important package deal for the NBA," said Toronto Raptors play-by-play man Chuck Swirsky. "The vision David Stern had was to have one team in the East—in a highly populated area that had many things going for it from a basketball standpoint—and one team in the West to generate another rivalry in the Northwest market."

From there, the two franchises went in opposite directions. While the Raptors showed improvement, reaching the playoffs for three straight seasons beginning in 2000, the Grizzlies posted an abysmal 101–359 record in Vancouver. The team was sold in 2000 to American businessman Michael Heisley, who moved the franchise to Memphis one year later.

Despite the Vancouver debacle, Stern declared the expansion into Canada a success. And with the steady growth of basketball interest in the country, it's hard to argue with him.

LIONEL CONACHER'S HALL-OF-FAME TRIFECTA (1963, 1966, 1994)

WHENEVER TWO-SPORT ATHLETES come along, sportswriters fawn over their ability to tackle two disciplines at a professional level.

Lionel Conacher might have laughed at such nonsense, not because he didn't respect two-sport athletes, but because two would have seemed like an awfully low number to a man who can lay claim to being the greatest athlete in Canadian history. Following his induction into the Canadian Football Hall of Fame (1963) and Canadian Lacrosse Hall of Fame (1966), Conacher entered rarefied air by joining the Hockey Hall of Fame in 1994, a trifecta that will likely never be duplicated.

In 1921, following championships in amateur wrestling and junior hockey, Conacher turned his attention to the Canadian Football League. To no one's surprise, he excelled immediately. The 21-year-old ran in a pair of touchdowns and even kicked a field goal as his Toronto Argonauts cruised past the Winnipeg Blue Bombers 23–0 in the first-ever East–West Grey Cup showdown.

The next year, Canada's national sport struck his fancy. In addition to leading the Argonauts to another successful playoff run, Conacher helped the Toronto Maitland lacrosse team capture the Ontario amateur championship, scoring four times and adding an assist in the 5–3 victory.

Having conquered several disciplines before his twenty-fifth birthday, Conacher set his sights on the National Hockey League. He thrived as a stay-at-home defenceman in a 12-year career with the Pittsburgh Pirates, New York Americans, Montreal Maroons, and Chicago Blackhawks. Conacher's career included three all-star nods, Stanley Cup titles in Chicago and Montreal, and even a stint as a player-coach with the Americans during the 1929–1930 season.

After being named Canada's athlete of the half-century in 1950, Conacher died of a massive heart attack in 1954 while trying to stretch a double into a triple during an annual baseball game between MPPs and the media. It surprised few that Conacher died doing what he had done his entire life, and it was this passion for sport that would see him recognized posthumously like no Canadian athlete before or since.

73

CANADA RETAINS ITS CUP (1991)

WAYNE GRETZKY HAD a simple goal for the 1991 Canada Cup: lead the host team to gold, no matter what.

Gretzky's words succeeded where his on-ice effort could not. With the world's greatest hockey player knocked silly, his teammates took up his cause, beating a pesky American team in the final to repeat as champions.

"Winning the Canada Cup was very special," said goaltender Bill Ranford. "My dad was in the military, so the biggest thing for me was just having the opportunity to represent my country."

After a sluggish start led to a 2–2 tie with Finland, Canada cruised through the rest of the round-robin with wins over the U.S., Sweden, and Czechoslovakia. The Canadians had already clinched first place in the division before their 3–3 draw with the Soviets to end the round-robin.

Canada rolled into the final with a 4–0 semifinal win over Sweden, behind the solid goaltending of Ranford. The Americans downed Finland 7–3 in the other semi, making the final an all-North American affair for the first time.

Canada scratched out a 4–1 win in the opener, though the result was an afterthought to most Canadians. Midway through the game, U.S. defenceman Gary Suter rammed Gretzky from behind, knocking "The Great One" hard into the boards. Gretzky went down in a heap, and wouldn't play again until the second month of the NHL season.

"There was plenty of initial frustration," said Ranford. "He had carried the team on his back. Initially, it affected us a lot, but luckily there were still leaders in the dressing room that helped us remain focused."

Canada rallied around Gretzky in Game 2, bursting out to a 2–0 lead. After the Americans drew even, a Suter giveaway sent Steve Larmer in on a shorthanded breakaway. He made no mistake, backhanding the puck past goaltender Mike Richter for the game-winner in a Cup-clinching 4–2 win.

The series wasn't as dramatic as the 1987 matchup with the Soviets, but that didn't matter to the Canadians. They had repeated as Canada Cup champions, just as Gretzky said they would.

The Canadian Press

RICHARD SCORES 5 IN HABS' PLAYOFF VICTORY (1944)

MAURICE RICHARD'S FIRST career NHL playoff game wasn't all that impressive. His second turned out to be one of the greatest performances in post-season history.

Richard's 32-goal season in 1943–1944 led a balanced Canadiens' attack, guiding the team to a spectacular 38–5–7 record. Their 83 points were 25 more than the runner-up Detroit Red Wings, making the Habs the overwhelming Stanley Cup favourite.

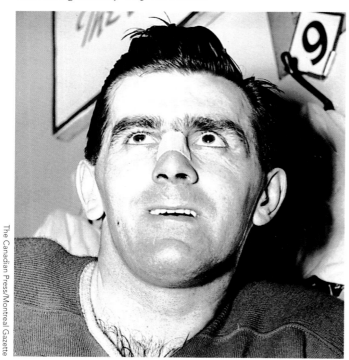

Hosting the Toronto Maple Leafs in the first round, the Canadiens fell victim to goaltender Paul Bibeault in a 3–1 opening-game loss, their first defeat on home ice all year. Bibeault turned aside 60 shots, including several off the stick of a frustrated Richard. The two had been friends since childhood, and while Richard applauded Bibeault's stunning Game 1 performance, he wasn't about to let his old pal show him up again.

Whatever worked for Toronto in the series opener did the trick in the first period two nights later, as Richard was kept off the score sheet once more. Fans became increasingly uneasy at the thought of the series returning to Maple Leaf Gardens with the Canadiens down 2–0.

Those worries melted away just over two minutes into the second period, by which time Richard had scored twice to give Montreal a 2–0 lead. After Toronto cut the lead to 2–1 at 8:50 in the period, "The Rocket" restored the two-goal advantage at 16:46. The crowd was abuzz, and Richard was hungry for more.

Richard added his fourth goal of the game one minute into the third period, bringing the Forum crowd to its feet once more. When he beat Bibeault for his record-setting fifth goal at 8:54, the game was stopped as teammates surrounded Richard to celebrate the moment. After the game, the 22-year-old was awarded first-, second-, and third-star honours.

Montreal wouldn't lose another game in the playoffs, winning seven straight while outscoring the Leafs and Chicago Blackhawks 38–11 the rest of the way to capture their fifth Stanley Cup title. Richard had arrived, all right, and with him came Montreal's triumphant return to hockey supremacy.

The Canadian Press/Montreal Gazette

The Canadian Press/Montreal Gazette

The Canadian Press/Paul Chiasson

KURT BROWNING LANDS SKATING'S FIRST QUAD (1988)

PLAGUED BY A HISTORY of second-place finishes, Kurt Browning decided it was his time to be first, and the ensuing result landed him in the *Guinness Book of World Records*.

After finishing runner-up to Brian Orser at the 1987 national championships, Browning added an original manoeuvre to his repertoire, the quadruple jump. Though he wouldn't be the first to practise it, he hoped to become the first skater to successfully execute one in actual competition.

"As soon as I learned to do a triple jump, it seemed natural to try a quad," said Browning (The Canadian Press, March 25, 1988).

The Albertan wasn't afraid to take a chance if it meant having a chance at victory. And true to form, Browning attempted his first quadruple jump at the 1987 Skate Canada competition. He failed to land it cleanly, and despite nailing seven triple jumps the rest of the way, he had to settle for a fourth-place finish.

Not wanting to squander his chance at making the Olympic team, Browning avoided a quad attempt at the 1988 Canadian championships, finishing second but doing well enough to qualify for the Calgary Games. There, he took another chance, and again he was unsuccessful.

The following month, at the world championships in Budapest, Browning vowed to make his third attempt a successful one. With all eyes on him, Browning launched himself into the air, completed four full rotations, and landed perfectly on one skate, becoming the first human to execute the jump in competition and earning himself a spot in the world's most famous book of records.

"It makes me very happy to think I got into the history of skating," Browning said (The Canadian Press, March 25, 1988).

Kurt left the quad as part of his free skate, and even added one to his short program, helping propel him to the 1989 world championship, his first of three world titles. Browning probably would have won without the quad, but by landing it, the innovative Canadian with the thirst for risk left no doubt that he was the best skater on the planet.

CANADA REACHES SOCCER'S WORLD CUP (1986)

CANADA'S FIRST AND ONLY appearance at the World Cup of soccer won't go down as the country's finest football moment, at least not to those who remember it.

How the Canadians managed to reach soccer's grandest stage—now, that's worth applauding.

"Given the stature that the World Cup holds right now, I think getting to the World Cup, and knowing I was a part of it, is probably the one achievement that stands out above the rest," said team member Bob Lenarduzzi.

Canada took advantage of its first two CONCACAF qualifying games in Victoria, blanking Haiti 2–0 and downing Guatemala 2–1. The Canadians followed with a 1–1 draw in Ciudad de Guatemala, leaving them needing a victory in Haiti three days later. Dale Mitchell and Igor Vrablic scored in a 2–0 win, and Canada was off to the CONCACAF final.

After drawing Costa Rica 1–1 in Toronto, the Canadian team embarked on its most difficult task yet—a date with the host Hondurans. Facing an especially hostile Tegucigalpa crowd, the Canadians stunned Honduras 1–0 on George Pakos's goal in the fifty-eighth minute.

The window for Honduras would remain open with a 3–1 win over the Costa Ricans, who had fought Canada to a scoreless draw one week earlier. Canada would advance to the World Cup with either a win or tie against the Hondurans in St. John's, Nfld.

Pakos gave Canada an early lead in the fifteenth minute. The Hondurans stormed back early in the second half, but Vrablic restored Canada's lead 12 minutes later, sparking jubilation from coast to coast. Canada held on for a 2–1 victory and a spot in the 1986 World Cup.

The team would wind up going winless and goalless in Mexico, but that didn't matter to Canadian fans or players.

"The fact that we didn't score, I don't think it's something that people really latched on to," said Lenarduzzi.

"We were competitive in every game we played.

"It was a wonderful experience, and one that I relive on a regular basis in my mind."

The Canadian Press/Montreal Gazette

CANADIENS RULE REGULAR SEASON (1976–1977)

NO TEAM IN NHL HISTORY has ever done more celebrating than the 1976–1977 Montreal Canadiens.

Stocked with future Hall of Famers at every position, the Canadiens ripped through the league in the late 1970s, winning four straight Stanley Cups in dominant fashion. The 1976–1977 edition was the most menacing of all, putting together the best regular-season performance in NHL history.

The Canadian Press/Doug Ball

"We could play any style," said defenceman Larry Robinson, one of the team's young stars. "We enjoyed being around each other and each guy drove the next guy to play better. We were a big family."

The Canadiens had finished 58–11–11 the year before, and with the core of the team intact, everyone was tabbing Montreal to repeat as champion. A 10–1 rout of the Pittsburgh Penguins on opening night served as a sign of things to come.

Montreal enjoyed one stretch where it would lose just once in 22 games (18–1–3), expanding its division lead to 28 points over the Penguins. Later in the season, the Canadiens went unbeaten over a 21-game stretch, leaving open an outside chance of becoming the first NHL team to win 60 games in a season.

With Montreal's 4–1 loss to Buffalo on March 6, the Canadiens needed to finish with 10 wins over their final 12 games to set the record. And that's exactly how they wound up the season—with 10 wins and two ties, reaching the 60-win plateau with a 2–1 victory over Washington in their regular-season finale. The Canadiens went 60–8–12 that season.

Montreal lost just twice in 14 post-season games to cruise to its second straight Stanley Cup title. The Canadiens would claim the championship in each of the next two seasons, finishing the four-year stretch from 1975 to 1979 with an otherworldly 229–46–45 mark in the regular season, and a 48–10 record in the playoffs.

Robinson had no trouble assessing the quality of the late-1970s Canadiens.

"To win four years in a row—and we came close to making it five—I'd have to say those were probably the best teams I've ever been on."

The Canadian Press

The Canadian Press/COC/Sandy Grant

LENNOX LEWIS FIGHTS HIS WAY TO GOLD (1988)

PATIENCE PAID OFF in gold for Lennox Lewis.

The English-born, Canadian-raised boxer went home empty-handed following a heartbreaking defeat at the 1984 Olympics in Los Angeles. Lewis made the difficult decision to retain his amateur status for another four years, and he was rewarded with a long-awaited gold medal at the 1988 Olympics in Seoul.

After dropping a controversial decision to Tyrell Biggs at the 1984 Games and having to settle for fifth, Lewis admits he nearly left his amateur boxing days behind.

"I was very close to turning pro," said Lewis. "A lot of promoters and people came after me then. But I was still young. It was my first Olympics, and I treated it like a learning experience.

"People asked me, 'Why wait four years when you might lose again?' But I was willing to take that chance."

Driven by the desire for gold, Lewis was a buzz saw in Seoul. He beat his opening-round opponent with a second-round TKO, and toppled his quarter-final adversary in the opening round. His semifinal opponent withdrew, sending Lewis into the final against American Riddick Bowe with fewer than three rounds of fighting under his belt.

Neither fighter seemed all that interested in taking control in a clutching, plodding first round. A frustrated Lewis took the fight to Bowe in Round 2, inducing a standing count in the first 25 seconds.

Moments later, Lewis staggered Bowe with a right hook to the side of the head, leading to a second standing count. The referee elected to stop the fight, and Lewis pranced around the ring, arms raised. The Olympic gold was finally his, and while he would later turn pro as a Briton, he was happy to flaunt his Canadiana in Seoul.

"When I was growing up and going to boxing tournaments, Canada was never considered a strong boxing nation," said Lewis. "And I always wondered, 'Why were all these other guys ranked ahead of me? Just because they came from another country?'

"So for that reason, it was great that I could win gold for Canada."

The Canadian Press

GILLES THE THRILL WINS AT HOME (1978)

THE ON-TRACK DEATH of Canadian auto-racing icon Gilles Villeneuve in 1982 brought shock but not surprise to the Formula One world.

In his five-year F1 career, Villeneuve was as daring as they come, never afraid to nudge opponents if it meant reaching the winner's circle. He died as he lived, and in 1978 he lived well, ending his first full F1 campaign with a victory at the Canadian Grand Prix in Montreal, not far from where he raced snowmobiles as a kid.

The Canadian Press

"On and off the track he was the same," said Gilles's son Jacques, a former F1 champion. "He fully lived his passion, and nothing else existed. He started racing because he loved not only driving fast, but driving faster than other people. That's just the way he was."

While Gilles Villeneuve struggled in his Ferrari for the first half of the 1978 season, his fortunes changed in the second half as he reeled off four straight top-eight finishes, highlighted by a third-place performance in Austria. Engine failure knocked Villeneuve out of the second-last race of the season, leaving him one final chance to earn his first career victory, the Canadian Grand Prix.

The excitement built to a crescendo in the days leading up to the race as fans scrambled to see one of their own behind the wheel. Opening third on the grid behind France's Jean-Pierre Jarier and Jody Scheckter of South Africa, Villeneuve found himself trailing Jarier well past the halfway mark of the race.

Then the unthinkable happened. Brake failure sent Jarier to the pits on Lap 50 and, when it was discovered that his car had an irreparable oil leak, his race came to an abrupt end. Villeneuve was alone in front, and he cruised the final 20 laps for a 13-second victory over Scheckter.

Villeneuve's storybook ending to the 1978 season had been written, giving fans something to remember well after his tragic death. The track was eventually re-named after him, providing a fitting homage to Canada's first—and possibly greatest—racing car legend.

The Canadian Press

66

ORR SCORES CUP WINNER FOR THE AGES (1970)

BOBBY ORR WAS KNOWN AS one of the fastest men on skates.

It's funny, then, that the Boston Bruins legend was actually hurtling through the air when he scored the most incredible of his 296 career NHL goals.

Orr's dramatic goal clinched the Bruins' sweep of the St. Louis Blues, giving Boston its first Stanley Cup championship in nearly three decades. Orr's shot, taken just as he was tripped by Blues defenceman Noel Picard, was immortalized in photos and on television highlights. Fans and media alike proclaimed it one of the greatest goals in league history.

The Bruins were the class of the Eastern Conference, matched against a St. Louis Blues team considered one of the weakest Stanley Cup entries in history. Boston was in the Stanley Cup for the first time since 1958, while the Blues were in their third straight final, having been swept in each of the previous two series.

Blues backup goalie Ernie Wakely, in for an injured Jacques Plante, found little sympathy from Orr, Phil Esposito, and the rest of the Bruins sharpshooters. Wakely allowed 12 goals in back-to-back losses to open the series, and the Bruins moved to within a win of the championship with a 4–1 victory in Game 3.

Boston players wanted to wrap up the series without having to return to St. Louis, but the Blues weren't so accommodating. The teams were tied 2–2 when Larry Keenan put St. Louis out in front early in the third period. Boston veteran Johnny Bucyk tied the game with seven minutes left, forcing overtime.

Orr ended the series 40 seconds into the extra period. Working a give-and-go with Derek Sanderson, Orr barrelled toward the net, taking Sanderson's return pass and directing the puck past Blues goalie Glenn Hall. A split second later, Orr glided into Picard's stick, sending him airborne, arms lifted high as he watched the puck find the net.

With that, the Bruins were champions once again, and the image of Orr soaring through the air became the signature of his decade-long NHL legacy.

65

The Associated Press/Gene J. Puskar

MARIO'S MAGNIFICENT RETURN (1993)

MARIO LEMIEUX WILL ALWAYS be known as a gifted playmaker and stickhandling artist, and one of the few players to revolutionize the NHL.

The Associated Press/Keith Srakocic

But Lemieux will also be remembered for what he accomplished in 1993, a feat that perhaps no player will ever duplicate: returning from cancer to win the unlikeliest of his six scoring titles with the Pittsburgh Penguins, and capturing the Hart Trophy as league MVP.

"This means a lot to me because of the adversity I went through," Lemieux said after accepting the award. "I feel pretty good" (The Canadian Press, June 17, 1993).

Lemieux began the season on a record tear, scoring 14 goals and adding 18 assists over the Penguins' first 10 games. By the mid-season pole, Lemieux was running away with the scoring lead.

On January 12, 1993, two days after a 3–2 loss to the Winnipeg Jets, Lemieux's world was torn to pieces. During a routine checkup for his ailing back, Lemieux pointed out a lump on his neck. A biopsy revealed that the growth was cancerous, and Lemieux began immediate radiation treatment. Hockey took a backseat; Lemieux was now fighting for his life.

The treatments rid Lemieux of the cancer, and after missing 23 games, he suited up just hours after his final radiation treatment. Lemieux returned in style, recording a goal and an assist in Pittsburgh's 5–4 loss in Philadelphia.

Two games later, Lemieux and the Penguins began a record-setting tear. Lemieux finished with 52 points over his final 20 games to win the Art Ross with 160 points (69 goals, 91 assists) in just 60 games. The Penguins rode the wave to a season-ending 17-game winning streak.

"What Mario Lemieux accomplished in a short time, well, everybody was stunned," said Pierre Page, then the head coach and general manager of the Quebec Nordiques. "I couldn't believe what he was doing" (The Canadian Press, June 17, 1993).

The Penguins suffered a second-round upset at the hands of the New York Islanders, but the loss did little to dampen spirits in Pittsburgh. The Penguins may have lost their crown, but they had their king back—alive and well.

The Associated Press/Don Heupel

The Associated Press/Bill Kostroun

VINCE CARTER WINS NBA SLAM DUNK TITLE (2000)

VINCE CARTER SURE KNOWS how to throw a coming-out party—just ask anyone who stopped by Oakland Arena on February 12, 2000.

On that Saturday afternoon, the Toronto Raptors swingman put on a dazzling display of dunking prowess en route to victory at the NBA slam-dunk competition. Carter's performance galvanized the reigning Rookie of the Year's status as a must-see attraction.

"It absolutely put Carter on the map," said Raptors play-by-play announcer Chuck Swirsky. "That victory really gave him an identity and moved him into another gear, and it helped establish the Raptors franchise as well."

Carter's participation in the slam-dunk event generated considerable buzz, particularly since there hadn't been a dunk competition in three seasons. Carter, teammate Tracy McGrady, and Houston Rockets leaper Steve Francis were considered the men to beat.

After opening with a vicious 360-degree reverse windmill, Carter followed with an equally ferocious reverse windmill from behind the basket, drawing perfect scores from the judges and looks of astonishment from fellow all-stars watching courtside.

Carter saved his best for the end of the first round. With McGrady dropping the perfect bounce pass, Carter caught the ball, sprang toward the hoop, and nailed a between-the-legs windmill. As Carter walked away from the basket, he had two words for the TV cameras: "It's over."

Carter was right: McGrady, Francis, and the rest of the high-flyers had no answer for the second-year sensation. Carter ended the competition with a one-handed slam that saw him hanging off the rim by his elbow, followed by a two-handed dunk from just inside the free-throw line. In the end, just about everyone ended up with something. Carter had another piece of NBA hardware, the league had a new slam-dunk champion—and Toronto Raptors fans had their saviour.

"I knew he was going to win after watching him practise his dunks," said Swirsky. "I thought to myself, 'If he can pull these off, he's going to win.'

"Sure enough, he brought the house down, and from that moment on, his world changed dramatically."

The Associated Press/Ben Margot

BOBBY ORR NAMED *SI'S* SPORTSMAN OF THE YEAR (1970)

BOBBY ORR'S spectacular 1969–1970 season was special for several reasons. His 120 points earned him the NHL scoring title, the first and only time that honour has gone to a defenceman. Orr also became the only man in history to capture four major trophies in one season: the Hart, Art Ross, Norris, and Conn Smythe awards.

Orr's year to remember also made history by making unprecedented noise south of the border, including a special nod from world-renowned magazine *Sports Illustrated*, which made the Boston Bruins megastar its Sportsman of the Year. It was the first time a hockey player had been honoured, and would help launch the NHL to never-before-seen levels of popularity.

Though the third-year blue-liner had already established himself as one of the league's brightest young stars, the 1969–1970 campaign served as his coronation as the greatest hockey player on earth. His 33 goals and 87 assists were records for a defenceman, and his 120 total points were just six short of the NHL single-season mark.

He would cap off his historic season by leading the Bruins to a four-game sweep of the St. Louis Blues for their fourth Stanley Cup championship and their first in 29 years. Orr fittingly scored the Cup-clinching goal, knocking the puck into the net while flying through the air in one of the most famous scoring plays in league history (honoured on page 48).

At the end of the calendar year, with Orr and the Bruins on pace to demolish scoring records, the 22-year-old hit the big time. There, with a rainbow array of colours in the background, Orr appeared in uniform on the cover of the December 21, 1970, issue of *Sports Illustrated*. Though he had appeared on the cover twice before, this time he was the Sportsman of the Year, joining such notable athletes as baseball Hall of Famers Stan Musial and Sandy Koufax, NBA great Bill Russell, and golf legend Arnold Palmer.

It was an incredible end to an incredible year for one of the most incredible talents to ever lace up a pair of skates.

SPORTSMAN OF THE YEAR 1970

BOBBY ORR

62

The Canadian Press/Globe and Mail/Tom Szlukovenyi

LIZ MANLEY SNAGS SILVER IN CALGARY (1988)

THE TWO SILVER MEDALS earned by Canada at the 1988 Winter Olympics in Calgary generated very different reactions from the athletes who won them.

For men's figure skater Brian Orser, a second-place finish left a bitter taste in his mouth after American Brian Boitano won the much-publicized "Battle of the Brians."

The Canadian Press/COC/C. McNeil

By contrast, Liz Manley's silver-medal performance left the Ottawa, Ont., native skating on a cloud. Manley, too, came within a whisper of capturing gold, but she was a long shot to even win a medal. For her, the second-place result was a blessing.

Despite claiming her third national title in 1988, Manley was not expected to win a medal in Calgary. Compounding her situation was a nasty illness that left her wondering if she would even be able to compete.

"I couldn't physically get through a run-through of a program," said Manley. "I just didn't have the strength. I

The Canadian Press/Edmonton Journal/Brian Gavriloff

was panicking—we would be competing at altitude, and I didn't think I would be able to fight through it."

Her short program changed things dramatically: with the boisterous Saddledome crowd behind her, Manley skated a near-flawless short program and found herself in third place.

As leaders Katarina Witt and Debi Thomas stumbled, Manley sent the home fans into hysterics with her long program, landing every triple jump while displaying her trademark verve. When the music ended, Manley covered her face with both hands as the crowd exploded into applause.

"I was in complete shock," said Manley. "At that point, I didn't even care if I won a medal. I had just skated the best routine of my life."

Manley won the free skate handily, finishing mere fractions behind Witt in the overall standings. Yet, unlike Orser, Manley certainly wasn't left disappointed. She was, in fact, the happiest person in the building.

"It was a bit of a rough Games for us, and I kind of ended things on a high note for the country," said Manley.

"To be able to say I ended my amateur career pleasing my country, that's like a medal in itself."

RCGA/Canadian Golf Hall of Fame archives

61

SANDRA POST WINS LPGA CHAMPIONSHIP (1968)

SANDRA POST'S VICTORY at the 1968 LPGA Championship wasn't just surprising, it was downright stunning.

Post earned her victory in style, beating American Kathy Whitworth in a playoff to shock the golf world by becoming the youngest woman to ever win a major. Post was the next big thing in women's golf, and remained one of Canada's greatest sports ambassadors throughout her 16-year career.

Post was barely 20 when she competed at the LPGA Championship in Worcester, Mass. Post put together a magnificent tournament, sharing the first-round lead and remaining in contention all week. A final-round even-par 73 left her 2 over for the tournament, good for a first-place tie with the legendary Whitworth.

"I called home right after the fourth round and told my parents, 'I have to play another 18 holes tomorrow, can you come down?'" said Post. "I don't get home until one or two in the morning, I get no sleep, and I figure I'm the runner-up for the LPGA Championship, which is still pretty good."

Post opened with two birdies and an eagle over her first four playoff holes, but Whitworth was equal to the task, beginning her round with four straight birdies. Yet, while Whitworth finally cooled off, Post continued her hot play, making a pair of challenging chip shots to open up a lead.

Post's defining moment came on the 16th, where she holed out a wedge from around 80 yards out. Two holes later, she completed a round of 5-under 68 to win by a whopping seven shots.

Post earned U.S. $3,000 for the win, along with instant respect around the golf world. As the youngest player to capture a major tournament, Post had a significant place in the LPGA annals. Her record would stand for nearly four decades, and her impact on the Canadian golf scene has lasted even longer.

"I've always been proud of the women golfers in this country," Post said. "If they point to me, saying I've inspired them, then I feel very grateful for that."

The Canadian Press/COC/Mike Ridewood

HEDDLE AND MCBEAN TRIPLE UP IN ATLANTA (1996)

WINNING A PAIR OF gold medals at the 1992 Summer Olympics seemed like a fitting way for rower Kathleen Heddle to end her career, but teammate Marnie McBean had a different plan in mind.

The Canadian Press/COC/Mike Ridewood

She coaxed Heddle out of retirement in 1994 and the two stroked their way into the record books, winning a third gold at the 1996 Olympics and adding a bronze to become the most decorated Canadian athletes in the Summer Games competition.

Heddle and McBean enjoyed their first international success at the 1991 world championships in Vienna, capturing gold in both the women's coxless pairs and the women's eights. The duo was brimming with confidence heading into the 1992 Summer Games in Barcelona, where they became instant Canadian heroes, edging out a German duo to capture gold in coxless pairs. They added a second gold as part of the women's eights.

Having reached the pinnacle of her sport, Heddle opted to leave rowing indefinitely. McBean wasn't ready to call it quits, and focused on a singles career in Heddle's absence. After failing to qualify for the 1994 world championships in Indianapolis, she sought another way in, and called Heddle.

The thrill of the challenge had become too difficult to resist, and Heddle agreed to come back on a trial basis. Neither rower knew what to expect, with the 1994 worlds less than two months away. Yet, after just seven weeks of preparation, the duo finished second in the final, less than a second behind New Zealand.

The 1996 Olympics featured one of the deepest fields in double sculls, but the Canadians, coming off a win at the 1995 worlds, proved equal to the task. The duo won a thrilling final, holding off a Chinese pair for top spot. For the first time in Olympic history, Canada had itself a pair of three-time gold medallists.

Heddle and McBean added a bronze in the women's eights, bringing their career Olympic haul to four medals apiece and allowing them to leave Georgia as Canada's uncontested queens of the Games.

The Canadian Press/COC/Mike Ridewood

The Canadian Press/John Lehmann

DAVE STIEB FINALLY GETS HIS NO-NO (1990)

IF MAJOR-LEAGUE BASEBALL games lasted just eight innings, former Blue Jays pitcher Dave Stieb would be the sport's no-hit king.

The right-hander with the knee-buckling curveball fashioned a solid career with the Jays, winning 175 games and making seven trips to the all-star game. But Stieb had become known more for his series of no-hit near-misses—three times Stieb lost a no-hitter with two outs in the ninth inning. In 1990, he finally joined the exclusive fraternity, holding the Cleveland Indians without a hit in a 3–0 win that provided the Jays with their first-ever no-hitter.

Stieb's run of near-misses began in 1988 when he held the Indians hitless through eight-and-two-thirds innings before Julio Franco dropped a single into centre field, spoiling the no-hit bid with one strike to spare. Six days later, Stieb ended up in the exact same place. Leading Baltimore 4–0, Stieb surrendered a hit to Jim Traber with two outs in the ninth, erasing another no-no.

The following season, lightning struck again. This time, Stieb was one out away from a perfect game when Yankees veteran Roberto Kelly hit a double down the left-field line.

Given his history, Stieb was cautious as he carried a no-hitter into the ninth inning of a game against Cleveland on September 2, 1990. A Chris James flyout and Candy Maldonado strikeout left Stieb in a familiar spot: one out away from a no-hit ledger.

Alex Cole drew a walk, sending Jerry Browne to the plate. Having lost a no-hitter in that very stadium almost two years earlier, Stieb took a little extra time between pitches. When Browne poked a harmless line drive to a waiting Junior Felix in right field, an elated Stieb was mobbed by his teammates.

Stieb acknowledged he wasn't at his best that day, but that didn't matter in the end. "I had much better stuff the other times, much better control," he said. "I always knew it took a lot of luck to get a no-hitter" (The Canadian Press, September 2, 1990).

CLEMENTS AND GABRIEL HOOK UP FOR GREY CUP (1976)

BETWEEN THE ROUGH RIDERS and Renegades leaving town and the Senators coming up short in their Stanley Cup quests, Ottawa sports fans haven't done much celebrating over the past three-plus decades.

Yet, for all the sports-related misery thrust upon it, Ottawa will always have the distinction of winning one of the most entertaining games in Grey Cup history, capped by a most improbable comeback orchestrated by second-year quarterback Tom Clements and star tight end Tony Gabriel.

"You definitely have to include this as one of the great games in the history of the Grey Cup," said Canadian Press football reporter Dan Ralph. "It was a classic."

Ottawa met Saskatchewan in a battle of the 'Riders before nearly 60,000 fans at Toronto's Exhibition Stadium. Gerry Organ put Ottawa out in front with a field goal before Bill Hatanaka made CFL history, returning a punt 79 yards for the score. It was the first punt return TD in Grey Cup history, and gave the East 'Riders a 10–0 advantage.

Saskatchewan took over in the second quarter, scoring 17 straight points on a Bob Macoritti field goal and touchdown passes to Steve Mazurak and Rob Richardson. The Western 'Riders were rolling, up 17–10 at the half.

Field goals provided the only scoring in the third quarter, and Saskatchewan nursed a 20–16 lead late in the game. After being stopped at the goal line on their previous possession, Ottawa had one last chance to win the game, sitting at Saskatchewan's 24-yard line with 20 seconds left.

While Saskatchewan wasn't fooled by Clements's fake handoff, the Rough Riders were caught flat-footed on Gabriel's ensuing fake post pattern, leaving him facing man-to-man coverage. Clements rolled out and lobbed the ball to Gabriel, who beat the defender and caught the ball in the end zone to give Ottawa the thrilling victory.

Gabriel's stunning grab is still talked about, especially in Ottawa, where fans revelled in what would end up being the final championship for the Rough Riders franchise. Decades later, the nation's capital is still waiting for its next major sports title.

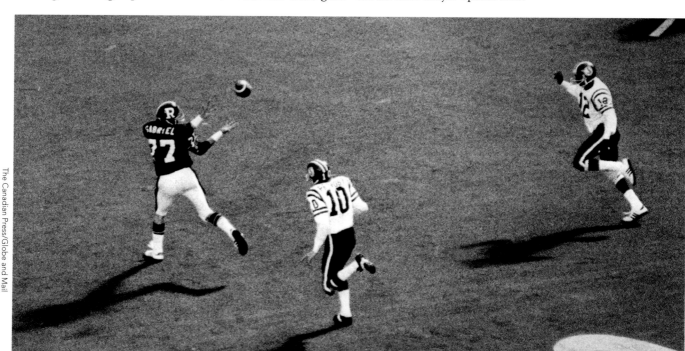

The Canadian Press/Ryan Remiorz

KERRIN LEE-GARTNER GRABS GOLD IN FRANCE (1992)

AS A YOUNG GIRL in Rossland, B.C., Kerrin Lee-Gartner had an opportunity to do something few people get to do. She touched an Olympic gold medal, all the while dreaming of winning her own.

The Canadian Press/Ryan Remiorz

Living two doors down from Canadian ski icon Nancy Greene afforded Lee-Gartner such a rare privilege. And thanks to support and advice from Greene, coupled with her rededication following two serious knee injuries, Lee-Gartner claimed her own prize in 1992, becoming the first Canadian to win gold in an Olympic downhill event.

"When my husband Al and I turned on the radio and heard there had been an upset win by Canada in the downhill, we sat up in bed and cheered," said Greene. "We jumped on the phone and started calling all our friends. It was really exciting."

Lee-Gartner entered the Albertville Games eager to improve upon her performances of four years earlier, when she finished no better than fifteenth in any discipline. Her recovery from a second serious knee surgery complete, Lee-Gartner was ready to build on the momentum of a strong World Cup season in her quest to reach the podium in France.

Gartner attacked the course, suffering a small slip-up on the top portion, but maintaining her balance and speed. Managing the second half of the course in expert fashion, Lee-Gartner was flawless, crossing the line in one minute, 52.55 seconds. That put her out in front by 0.12 over Katja Seizinger of Germany.

American Hilary Lindh posed the biggest threat, but ultimately came up short, finishing in 1:52.61. Veronika Wallinger of Austria was a close third in 1:52.64. And that left Lee-Gartner on top of the podium, finally reaching the pinnacle of her sport after years of rehab, recuperation, disappointment, and self-doubt.

For Lee-Gartner, the victory wouldn't have been possible without a little inspiration from the woman who lived two doors down.

"We've definitely touched each other," said Greene. "It's amazing how strong the bond is—not only between Kerrin and I, but between all Canadian female skiers, from one generation to another."

The Canadian Press/COC

The Canadian Press/Ray Giguere

CANADA COMPLETES JUNIOR HOCKEY'S "DRIVE FOR FIVE" (1997)

CANADIAN PRIDE TOOK a major hit when the national junior hockey team plummeted to a sixth-place finish in the 1992 world championship in Fussen, Germany.

The stunning result proved to be the turning point for the Canadian junior hockey program, culminating with a fifth consecutive title in Switzerland in 1997. No team had won five straight titles since Canada first began sending a national team to the tournament, and no team has done it since.

The Canadian Press/Ray Giguere

"It was an unbelievable experience and an unbelievable team," defenceman Jesse Wallin said after the squad was named team of the year by The Canadian Press. "We faced a lot of adversity going into that tournament and we used it to our advantage. There were a lot of knocks against us. We pushed ourselves to prove people wrong" (The Canadian Press, December 30, 1997).

The Canadian team looked shaky at times during the round-robin, settling for two wins and two ties in four games. Though it had secured a spot in the quarter-finals, the team knew it would have to play better—and fast—if it had any hope of defending its title.

Canada accomplished its mission the very next game, blasting Slovakia 7–2 behind goals from seven different players. Canada carried the momentum into a tightly contested 3–2 win over Russia, setting up a championship showdown with the U.S.

The Americans dominated play, beating Canada to most loose pucks and outshooting the defending champions 35–23. Those advantages were negated by the goaltending of Marc Denis, who was sensational in Canada's title-clinching 2–0 win. Boyd Devereaux scored midway through the second period to give the Canadians the lead, and Brad Isbister put the game away with a third-period goal.

Canada may not have played its best in 1997, but it was still the best in the world.

"It's a great honour to have coached the team and won, and everything that comes with it is fantastic," said head coach Mike Babcock. "All I think about when I hear the Canadian anthem is that moment" (The Canadian Press, December 30, 1997).

The Canadian Press/Dave Buston

JACQUES VILLENEUVE WINS INDIANAPOLIS 500 (1995)

GILLES VILLENEUVE WOULD HAVE been proud, and probably a little jealous.

Villeneuve, one of auto racing's most competitive drivers, enjoyed a successful Formula One career before perishing in a 1982 crash in Belgium. Thirteen years later, his son Jacques accomplished what no Canadian had done before him, capturing the prestigious Indianapolis 500.

A runner-up in his first Indy the year before, Villeneuve had a solid qualifying session and would start fifth on the grid behind Scott Brayton, Arie Luyendyk, Toronto's Scott Goodyear, and Bryan Herta.

Goodyear burst out to the immediate lead, with Villeneuve remaining in the hunt until passing his fellow Canadian on Lap 36. He would relinquish the lead to Michael Andretti three laps later, and Villeneuve stayed in hot pursuit until disaster struck on Lap 45. A crew mix-up saw the St-Jean-sur-Richelieu, Que., native pass the pace car twice during yellow flags, earning him a costly two-lap penalty, which dropped him to twenty-fourth place.

"Believe it or not, it actually made for a more fun race," said Villeneuve. "I realized I would have to drive more aggressively after that. Usually the Indy isn't a race you race hard at … you pick your spots. But I knew I would have to fight hard the whole race, not just at the end."

Villeneuve used yellow flags and pit stops to his advantage, working his way through the field until he regained the lead on Lap 156. He, Goodyear, and Scott Pruett duelled until Lap 185, when Pruett crashed into the wall while trying to challenge Goodyear.

On the ensuing restart, Goodyear jumped out ahead of the pace car in an effort to stave off the hard-charging Villeneuve. Having learned his lesson, Jacques held steady. Goodyear was black-flagged on Lap 193, taking him out of the running.

That left smooth sailing for Villeneuve, who sped across the finish line two and a half seconds ahead of runner-up Christian Fittipaldi.

"It was an amazing achievement," said Villeneuve. "With everything that had gone wrong, having to battle back the way we did made it that much sweeter."

The Associated Press/Mark Duncan

JUSTIN MORNEAU WINS AL MVP AWARD (2006)

IT TOOK LONGER than expected, but Justin Morneau's breakout season was well worth the wait.

The Minnesota Twins first baseman blasted his way into Canadian sports history, winning the 2006 American League Most Valuable Player award. He joined fellow B.C. native Larry Walker as the only Canadians to ever capture the award, and he was the first to turn the trick in the AL.

The Associated Press/Jim Mone

Morneau was coming off a 2005 campaign that saw him post just 22 home runs and 79 RBIs, numbers well below expectations. When Morneau came out struggling the following season, batting .202 in early May, whispers of "bust" made the rounds.

Morneau insisted he was fine, and proved it in shocking fashion. Between May and August 2006, Morneau was the best hitter in baseball, swatting 27 homers and knocking in 95 runs while batting .336. He hit even higher (.342) in September, adding another 19 RBIs to his total.

At season's end, Morneau had the kind of numbers the Twins envisioned when they promoted him to full-time status: a .321 batting average, 34 home runs, and 130 RBIs. In one of the closest votes in history, he beat

out New York Yankees shortstop Derek Jeter to win the MVP award.

What likely tipped the scales in Morneau's favour was Minnesota's unbelievable run to the pennant, which coincided with Morneau's surge. Mired at 25–33 in early June, the Twins finished the year on a 71–33 run, winning 96 games to finish atop the AL Central.

"That run that he was on that helped power the Twins to the AL Central was just unbelievable," said Canadian Press baseball writer Shi Davidi. "He just carried that team.

"There were great contributions from [teammates] Johan Santana and Joe Mauer, but the one consistent thing that they really needed from him and that he gave them was that power threat in the middle of the lineup."

Morneau was later congratulated by Walker, and recalled meeting the retired outfielder prior to his first major-league game. Walker sent Morneau a bat, which read: "To Justin, make Canada proud."

Just three years later, Morneau did exactly that.

The Associated Press/Kathy Willens

The Canadian Press

EDMONTON OILERS BEGIN HIGH-OCTANE DYNASTY (1984)

WHEN IT CAME TO SCORING GOALS, nobody did it better than the Edmonton Oiler teams of the 1980s.

Wayne Gretzky routinely scored 200 points a season. His wingers were perennial 50-goal scorers. Top defenceman Paul Coffey outscored most National Hockey League forwards.

Many believed it was only a matter of time before the Oilers captured the Stanley Cup. And after going through the requisite growing pains one year earlier, Edmonton did the expected in 1984, winning the first of their five championships.

The 1982–1983 Oilers had free-wheeled their way to an outstanding regular season, but the defending-champion New York Islanders had the perfect tonic: punishing defencemen and solid goaltending. The Islanders swept the inexperienced Oilers to capture their fourth straight Stanley Cup title.

"The Oilers were so much fun to watch," said national hockey columnist Al Strachan. "But that lost Cup was a real eye-opener for them. It made them realize that they would have to pay more attention to defence."

The Oilers rocketed out of the gate the following season, winning a franchise-record 57 games and scoring an unbelievable 446 goals en route to a Stanley Cup rematch with the Islanders. Edmonton netminder Grant Fuhr out-duelled future Hall of Famer Billy Smith in a 1–0 victory in Game 1, while the Islanders responded with a 6–1 thumping in Game 2.

The next three games were scheduled for Edmonton, giving the Oilers a chance to build some momentum. They ended up doing one better, posting back-to-back 7–2 victories in Games 3 and 4 before bringing the Islanders' dynasty to an end with a 5–2 win in the Cup clincher.

The Oilers won three more Cups in the decade and added a fifth in 1990. And while other NHL dynasties will inevitably come and go, few will be able to match the star power and goal-scoring prowess of the high-flying Oilers.

"It will be difficult to duplicate what the Oilers did," said Strachan. "Players who become dominant stars today are now too expensive to keep.

"It's going to be very difficult for any team to do that again."

The Canadian Press/Tom Hanson

MYRIAM BEDARD GOES DOUBLE GOLD IN BIATHLON (1994)

IN 1986, THE INTERNATIONAL Olympic Committee voted to separate the Summer and Winter Olympics, beginning in 1994. The scheduling anomaly left just a two-year space between the 1992 Winter Games in Albertville, France, and the 1994 Games in Lillehammer, Norway.

Few athletes took greater advantage of the smaller gap than Myriam Bedard, whose career peak just happened to coincide with the Lillehammer Olympics. The result: North America's first-ever biathlon gold medal, followed shortly by its second.

Despite enjoying a successful junior career, Bedard was not considered a medal favourite entering the 1992 Winter Games. To reach the podium, Bedard would have to be at her best—and she was, skiing a spectacular 15-kilometre race to finish third, six seconds ahead of Veronique Claudel of France. Bedard had an Olympic medal, Canada's first in biathlon.

The following year saw the Neufchatel, Que., native win the 7.5-kilometre sprint at the world championships, while adding a second-place finish in the 15-kilometre event. Having entered the 1992 Games as a virtual unknown, Bedard had quickly become one of the racers to beat in Norway.

After working on her fitness and stamina in the months leading up to the Games, Bedard left the competition in the dust in the 15-kilometre race, posting a time of 52 minutes, 6.6 seconds, 47 seconds faster than runner-up Anne Briand of France. No Canadian or American had ever stood atop the podium at an Olympic biathlon event until then.

Five days later, Bedard took part in the 7.5-kilometre event. Disaster struck when Bedard realized she had been wearing two differently waxed skis, and she trailed for the majority of the race before staging the most improbable of rallies, grinding through the snow in a furious

finish that saw her cross the line just over a second faster than Svetlana Paramygina of Belarus.

Bedard snagged her second gold of the Games to become the undisputed queen of the biathlon world. And thanks to a once-in-a-lifetime Olympic quirk, Bedard needed just 24 months to go from bronze-medal winner to double-gold champion.

The Canadian Press/COC/Ted Grant

The Associated Press/Mark J. Terrill

ERIC GAGNE GRABS NL CY YOUNG AWARD (2003)

WITH STARTING PITCHERS hogging the spotlight, it's difficult for a closer to even be considered for baseball's Cy Young Award.

Mascouche, Que., native Eric Gagne was one of the lucky ones. The hard-throwing right-hander captured the 2003 National League Cy Young trophy by putting together one of the most dominant performances by a reliever in the history of the sport.

The Associated Press/Roy Dabner

"I called my wife, I called my whole family, I called my friends," Gagne said shortly after winning the award. "Everybody was so happy about it. It was a great feeling" (The Canadian Press, November 13, 2003).

Gagne began the 2002 season as a closer after the Los Angeles Dodgers decided to convert him from his role as a starter. The move sent Gagne's career into orbit:

He finished with 52 saves, a 1.97 ERA, and 114 strikeouts in just 82-and-a-third innings. Gagne wound up finishing fourth in voting for the Cy Young, and twelfth in the NL Most Valuable Player race.

He was even more dominant in 2003.

After recording eight saves in April, Gagne saved all 11 Dodger victories in May. By the end of June, he had 29 saves. After allowing a run in a July 2 loss to San Diego, Gagne would give up just one more the rest of the season.

By season's end, the numbers were staggering: an NL record-tying 55 saves to go with a 1.20 ERA and 137 strikeouts, a record for a full-time reliever.

Gagne picked up 28 of a possible 30 first-place votes to become the first reliever in 11 years to win the Cy Young. He also joined Hall of Famer Ferguson Jenkins as the only Canadians to take home baseball's top pitching honour.

Gagne hopes that, by setting records on the mound, he has set an example for Canadian youth who might want to follow in his footsteps one day.

"I just hope that the kids are going to look up to me and say, 'OK, one day I want to be there, I want to be like Eric Gagne, I want to make it'" (The Canadian Press, November 13, 2003).

The Canadian Press/Ian Barrett

GRETZKY HITS THE SCORE SHEET IN 51 STRAIGHT (1984)

OF ALL THE NHL RECORDS Wayne Gretzky owns, even "The Great One" admits this one might be the toughest one to break.

The league's greatest scorer fashioned one of the greatest records of all time, scoring at least one point in 51 straight games. The feat stands alongside Joe DiMaggio's 56-game hitting streak and Johnny Unitas's 47 straight games with a touchdown pass as marks of consistency that may never be matched.

"This record's a tough break," said Gretzky. "In other sports, you can miss a game and your streak will stay intact. In hockey, you miss a game and it's over.

"So not only do you have to perform every night, you also have to be able to battle through injury."

Gretzky hit the score sheet with a bang, registering seven straight multi-point games to start the 1984–1985 campaign and equalling a career high with seven points in game No. 15, an 8-5 win over Winnipeg. Six games later, he had eight points in a 13–4 rout of New Jersey.

Gretzky blew past his previous high of 31 straight games with a point, and after putting together a dominant December, scoring 25 points in one six-game stretch, he reached the 50-game plateau January 25 against Vancouver.

Gretzky made it to No. 51 in the Oilers' next game against the Devils, leaving it next up to the Los Angeles Kings to end the streak. The Kings' only advantage was that Gretzky had suffered an injury to his right shoulder a week earlier, limiting his mobility.

The Kings' defence blanketed Gretzky for the majority of the game and, despite playing most of the final five minutes, he couldn't muster anything. The Kings went on to win 4–2, and Gretzky was held scoreless for the first time all season.

Gretzky proved to be mortal that night, but not before etching another entry in the NHL record books, one

that has as much staying power as any of his other lofty benchmarks.

"I think I was a little lucky along the way," said Gretzky, "but I'm very proud of the record."

EDMONTON ESKIMOS WIN FIFTH STRAIGHT GREY CUP (1982)

WARREN MOON WASN'T in the CFL for long, but his impact on the league remains as indelible as any player before or since.

Moon helped shape the Edmonton Eskimos into an unstoppable force in the late 1970s and early 1980s, leading the perennial West Division powerhouses to four straight championships. And, in one of the greatest performances by a quarterback in Grey Cup history, Moon single-handedly dismantled the Toronto Argonauts in the rain-soaked 1982 title game, giving Edmonton its fifth consecutive Grey Cup.

The Winnipeg Blue Bombers did everything they could to end Edmonton's streak in the West final. Were it not for a pair of late field-goal misses from Winnipeg kicker Trevor Kennerd, Manitoba would have been celebrating a berth in the Grey Cup. Instead, the Eskimos squeaked out a 24–21 victory to set up a Grey Cup meeting with the pesky Argonauts in their own backyard, Exhibition Stadium. Toronto had gone from worst to first in the East, earning its first win over Edmonton in eight years and obliterating Ottawa 44–7 in the division final.

The Argos burst out to an early lead on an 84-yard touchdown pass from Condredge Holloway to Emanuel Tolbert. Holloway would later find Terry Greer for a 10-yard score, and Toronto would enjoy a 14–10 lead.

The skies opened up soon after, and Moon became unstoppable. He guided the Eskimos to a lead they wouldn't relinquish, capped by his second TD pass of the game. Neil Lumsden ran in another Edmonton score, and Dave Cutler iced it with three straight field goals. Edmonton posted a 32–16 victory, wrapping up an unprecedented fifth straight title while leaving the Argos in search of their first title in 30 years.

The "Rain Bowl" drew the largest television audience in Canadian history at that time, enhancing Moon's profile to the point that he would bolt the league for the NFL in 1984. Eight CFL franchises—and the tens of thousands of fans rooting for each of them—were happy to see him go.

ELVIS STOJKO GOES THREE-FOR-FOUR AT SKATING WORLDS (1997)

IF A SINGLES FIGURE SKATER finds himself outside the top three after his short program, he almost certainly won't be going home with a gold medal.

Elvis Stojko found himself in such a predicament at the 1997 world figure skating championships in Lausanne, Switzerland. Then, in one of the most dramatic comebacks in the history of the event, Stojko skated a flawless long program while those ahead of him stumbled and fell.

The stunning turn of events earned Stojko his third world championship in four years, placing him alongside Kurt Browning as Canada's only three-time champions.

While Stojko was as technically sound as anyone, his kung-fu–inspired program was largely lost on judges, who penalized Stojko for executing what they considered to be a less artistic form of skating. Nowhere was this more evident than in Lausanne, where Stojko skated a clean and dynamic short program but ended up in fourth place behind rivals Alexei Urmanov, Ilya Kulik, and Todd Eldridge.

"My first thought was, 'What's the deal with this?'" said Stojko. "I watched the other skaters, and I knew I had skated better than they did. It was baloney. But if [the judges] wanted to play this game, no problem. I wasn't going to be denied."

Aside from a few wobbles, Stojko was masterful in the free skate, hitting eight triples and completing the first quadruple-triple combination in the history of the world championships. For that, Stojko earned a 6.0 score from one judge and 5.9s from the other eight. Whatever disadvantage Stojko faced in artistic impression had been negated by technical marks that could not be topped.

"I went out, set a world record, and skated clean," said Stojko. "And I knew that would put the pressure on Eldridge, and he would fold.

"I knew my competitors really well."

Eldridge followed through, tumbling while attempting a double Axel. Moments later, Stojko was world champion again, and he didn't care that it took some sloppy skating from his competition to help make it happen. For the third time, Stojko was the best male figure skater on the planet.

The Canadian Press/Montreal Gazette

MAURICE RICHARD'S CALMING INFLUENCE (1955)

THE MAURICE RICHARD RIOTS at the end of the 1954–1955 NHL season cast a pall on the league that would not dissipate for several years.

Yet, out of the carnage came a moment that would forever change the province of Quebec. The Canadiens' hero, Maurice Richard, took to the airwaves and pleaded for an end to the imbroglio. The chaos dissipated, and Richard instantly became the central figure in an incident many believe was the catalyst for Quebec's Quiet Revolution.

The maelstrom began four days earlier, when the Canadiens visited the Boston Bruins. A high stick from Bruins defenceman Hal Laycoe opened a gash on Richard's head. The fiery forward retaliated, slashing Laycoe over his face and shoulders until his stick broke. When official Cliff Thompson intervened, Richard punched him in the face, knocking him unconscious.

League president Clarence Campbell came down on Richard in unprecedented fashion. Citing previous acts of aggression, Campbell suspended "The Rocket" for the remainder of the regular season and playoffs.

Montreal fans bombarded call-in shows, demanding Campbell's head. Despite repeated threats to his well-being, Campbell attended the Canadiens' next home game against the Detroit Red Wings. He was promptly greeted by a torrent of eggs and garbage.

With Detroit leading 4–1, the fans began tossing debris on the ice. A smoke bomb exploded shortly after, forcing an evacuation and leading Campbell to declare the game a Detroit victory by forfeit. The brouhaha quickly spilled out onto the streets.

Hoping to make things right, Richard made a surprise radio appearance, telling fans he had accepted his fate. Richard then pleaded for calm, asking fans to "get behind the team and help the boys win" their series against the Rangers and Red Wings. The next day, peace prevailed.

Richard insisted he was "a hockey player, not a politician." His most ardent fans saw him as both and a whole lot more.

"People recognize what he did, especially the French-Canadians from that time," Jean Roy, Richard's friend and agent, said shortly after Richard's death in 2000.

The Canadian Press/Toronto Star

The Associated Press/Don Heupel

AL BALDING MAKES HISTORY WITH PGA WIN (1955)

MOST PGA GOLFERS get an early start on their careers.

Jack Nicklaus took up the sport at age 10, Mike Weir was just seven when he whacked balls around a par-three course, and Tiger Woods was a child prodigy, shooting a 48 over nine holes as a three-year-old.

The Canadian Press

It all makes Al Balding's achievement that much more amazing. Despite not discovering the sport until his early 20s, Balding won the 1955 Mayfair Open in Sanford, Fla., to become the first Canadian to ever win a PGA event.

"For him to get himself to a level where he could compete with other professionals in such a short amount of time says a lot about his determination more than anything," said longtime golf reporter Bob Weeks.

"He just knew how a golf swing worked."

Balding didn't begin swinging the clubs until after he returned from World War II. He took a job at a Burlington, Ont., golf course, where he first learned to play the sport, and before long, he was hooked.

After four years as an assistant professional, Balding moved up to head pro in 1954. The following year, he took on a full field of professionals at the Mayfair Open. Relying on pinpoint accuracy from just about everywhere on the course, Balding cruised to victory, earning a cheque for U.S. $2,400, a sizable payday at the time.

Balding finished his career with four PGA victories, and went on to enjoy a successful senior career, at one point shooting a whopping 12 strokes below his age.

"He kept himself in remarkable shape," said Weeks. "He worked out rigorously at a time when most people saw golf as a time when you could drink and smoke. That clearly helped him later in life."

Balding died of cancer in 2006 at the age of 82, remaining an avid golfer right until the end. Having missed out on the sport for the first 20 years of his life, it's fair to say Balding was simply making up for lost time.

The Associated Press

The Canadian Press

45

MARILYN BELL TAMES LAKE ONTARIO (1954)

MARILYN BELL had her doubts.

The 16-year-old long-distance swimmer didn't know whether or not she could handle 52 kilometres of choppy seas, high winds, and debilitating fatigue while an entire country followed her every stroke. Her goal was simply to last longer than her counterpart, American Florence Chadwick, even if she couldn't finish.

The Associated Press

Bell not only beat Chadwick, she left her a distant memory in the freezing confines of Lake Ontario, becoming the first woman to cross the enormous body of water, swimming from New York to Toronto in just under 21 hours. The heroic achievement generated international headlines, and made Bell a household name in Canada.

Chadwick entered Lake Ontario from Youngstown, N.Y., at around 11 p.m. on September 8, while Bell joined in roughly five minutes later. Fellow Canadian marathoner Winnie Roach, the first Canadian to cross the English Channel, also took part. The three swam into the darkness as a light rain fell on rigid waves. This would be no easy feat, even for the most accomplished long-distance swimmer.

While Chadwick and Roach were forced to withdraw around dawn, Bell remained in the water, though the overnight swim had taken its toll on her as well. She became so bewildered that at times she found herself briefly swimming the wrong way. By sunrise, with fatigue at its worst and the shoreline still not in sight, Bell believed she might have to withdraw. She had already beaten Chadwick, accomplishing her initial goal.

Bell's coach Gus Ryder spurred her to continue, and she did. As land approached, hundreds of thousands of fans stood at the shoreline, waiting for Bell's arrival. At 8:15 p.m. on September 9, Bell hit the breakwater, completing the swim in 20 hours, 59 minutes.

Bell was so disoriented that she didn't even acknowledge the crowds cheering her on. And after watching the diminutive teenager become the first person, man or woman, to swim across Lake Ontario, the fans were in a bit of a daze themselves. Nobody knew how she had done it. Everyone was simply ecstatic that she had.

The Canadian Press

The Canadian Press/Paul Chiasson

KURT BROWNING RULES SKATING WORLD (1993)

IT TOOK QUITE A WHILE for Canada to produce a four-time world men's figure-skating champion.

Having risen to international prominence far later than their international counterparts, Canadian skaters faced an uphill battle from the outset. Kurt Browning changed all that at the 1993 worlds in Prague, using a Casablanca-themed free skate to become the first Canadian to earn membership in one of the sport's most exclusive clubs.

Browning's main competitor in Czechoslovakia was countryman Elvis Stojko, just 20 but quickly gaining ground. Stojko's jump-happy style and herky-jerky artistry stood in complete contrast to Browning's carefully choreographed routines.

"Elvis was intimidating, and it wasn't as much fun to compete against Elvis," Browning said at his World Figure Skating Hall of Fame induction in 2006. "Elvis was like, you didn't sleep the night before" (The Canadian Press, March 23, 2006).

Kurt skated a clean, short program, vaulting to the top of the standings with American Mark Mitchell sitting a surprising second. Russia's Alexei Urmanov was third, and Stojko, who made little impression on the judges, sat fourth.

Browning transformed himself into Humphrey Bogart for the free skate, performing the same Casablanca routine that had earned him the Canadian title. The program was a hit, especially to Browning.

"Casablanca was the kind of program that made me relax in competition because there was a character involved," Browning said shortly before turning pro in 1994.

Browning hit the ice dancing, his fancy footwork bringing the crowd out of its seats. Though his program wasn't a clean one, his artistic marks made up for the shortfall. Browning captured the free skate, sweeping both programs to earn his fourth world title.

Stojko leapt his way into second, landing eight triple jumps to finish second in the long program. Canadians were 1–2 in men's singles just one night after Isabelle Brasseur and Lloyd Eisler won gold for Canada in pairs. Prague was awash in red and white, and the figure-skating world along with it.

Browning is one of just eight male performers to win four world championships, and with competition as level as it has ever been, it may be a while before another skater joins the club.

The Canadian Press/Paul Chiasson

43

CRAZY CANUCKS ROCK THE SKI HILLS (1974–1984)

IT WAS ENOUGH to make European skiing fans nervous.

A formidable group of Canadian downhillers knocked the sport on its ear, putting together a decade-long string of daring and dominant performances. Together, these "Crazy Canucks"—Jim Hunter, Ken Read, Dave Irwin, Dave Murray, and Steve Podborski—challenged the world's most dangerous hills and lived to tell about it.

The team first began making headway in the 1974 season, with Murray posting a ninth-place finish at the world championships and Hunter narrowly missing the podium in Val d'Isere. The following year, the quintet littered the hills with top-20 results, and the locals were beginning to take notice. The Canadians were a haphazard bunch, zipping down the hills at breakneck speeds. And they were succeeding.

"There was a great deal of shock at the beginning," said Podborski. "But we had a great deal of support from the other countries … mostly because we were everyone's second-best team.

"When we went to France, the fans there wanted us to finish second behind the French skiers. It was better, to them, than seeing the Austrians or Germans finish second."

On December 7, 1975, Read bolted down the Val d'Isere course in two minutes, 4.97 seconds, then held on for Canada's first-ever World Cup downhill victory. Two weeks later, Irwin outpaced the field at Schladming, Austria, by a whopping two seconds.

On Boxing Day 1978, Canada enjoyed one of its greatest moments on the slopes, placing four skiers in the top 10 at the Schladming course. The "Crazy Canucks" had reached the pinnacle of the sport and, more importantly, they had done so as a cohesive unit.

The team would finish 15 World Cup wins, 40 podium results, and an Olympic bronze medal courtesy of Podborski, providing Canadians with immense pride in their national ski program, and inspiration for the country's next generation of skiers.

"My goal, selfishly, has always been to help Canada kick you-know-what," Podborski joked. "Those were good times for me. And it's heartening that people still remember them in a positive light."

The Canadian Press/Fred Chartrand

GREG'S SILVER-MEDAL JUMP FOR JOY (1976)

THE 1976 SUMMER OLYMPICS in Montreal was not one of the country's finest moments.

The 16-day Games left the city with a paralyzing debt, a stadium that wasn't completed until after the Olympics left town, and plenty of bitterness toward Mayor Jean Drapeau, who vowed the Games would not produce a deficit. It didn't help that Canada became the first host nation to go without a gold medal at its own Summer Olympics.

The Canadian Press/COC/RW

Yet, for all the negativity the Montreal Games produced, there were some positives, none more profound than Greg Joy's silver-medal performance in the high jump. Given the surprising nature of the result—and the fact that it came at the expense of an American jumper who had allegedly bashed French-Canadians earlier in the Games—Joy's silver was as good as gold to Canadians in attendance.

A pair of Canadians, Joy and Claude Ferragne, had reached the final, though Ferragne was eliminated early

on. That left Joy, born in Portland, Ore., but raised in Vancouver, to bring Canada its first gold medal of the Games on the second-last day of competition. A steady rain during the final made things even more challenging for the jumpers, ensuring American Dwight Stones's world record of 2.31 metres would likely remain intact.

Stones could only manage a jump of 2.21 metres in the final. It was the same height he leapt at the 1972 Summer Games in Munich, West Germany. And it yielded the same result: a disappointing bronze medal. Joy would leap 2.23 metres—second only to Jacek Wszola of Poland (2.25)—to earn Canada's fifth silver of the Games, and its first track and field medal since the 1964 Games in Tokyo.

Joy was chosen to carry Canada's flag at the closing ceremony, a tremendous honour for the 20-year-old. He later took home the Canadian Male Athlete of the Year award, capping a year in which he provided one of the only highlights for an Olympic Games fraught with problems.

The Canadian Press/COC/RW

The Canadian Press/Andre Forget

SALÉ AND PELLETIER GET THEIR GOLD (2002)

JAMIE SALÉ AND DAVID PELLETIER just wanted to win the pairs competition at the 2002 Olympics in Salt Lake City.

In the end, four skaters wore gold medals around their necks, and grudges against those who tarnished their Olympic experience.

The Canadian Press/HO/COC/Andre Forget

The now-infamous event began February 11, 2002, with the pair's free skate. Russian skaters Elena Berezhnaya and Anton Sikharulidze were out in front, but their lead was a small one after the pair skated an underwhelming program, including a botched double Axel by Sikharulidze.

Salé and Pelletier knew a clean performance would mean gold. They remained calm and collected while the pro-Canadian crowd urged them on to a flawless skate. The majority in attendance believed Salé and Pelletier were the winners.

The majority was wrong.

While the technical merit scores put Salé and Pelletier ahead, the artistic impression marks were shockingly low, so much so that they were greeted with a wave of boos that lasted nearly a minute. The stunning turn of events allowed Berezhnaya and Sikharulidze to hang on to the lead and capture the gold medals.

The Canadian duo couldn't mask its frustration while receiving the silver medals. As Salé wept, Pelletier stood sombrely, then tore off his medal when the ceremony was over. The ISU launched an immediate investigation into the possibility of fixed judging at the pair's competition.

All eyes focused on French judge Marie-Reine Le Gougne, who confessed in an ISU review session the next day that she had been pressured by French federation president Didier Gailhaguet to favour the Russian tandem. Le Gougne was suspended, the ISU promised wide-sweeping changes to the marking system, and Salé and Pelletier were recognized as co–gold medallists.

"Obviously we would rather have won it that night," Salé said, "because of the pride and the joy of standing on the podium. Since I was a youngster, I had visualized myself being on top of the podium and seeing the flag come down and hearing the national anthem. Ask any athlete and that is what they dream of" (The Canadian Press, February 7, 2006).

The Canadian Press/Frank Gunn

DARRYL SITTLER'S PERFECT 10 (1976)

THE GREATEST SINGLE-GAME performance in NHL history doesn't belong to Wayne Gretzky, Mario Lemieux, Gordie Howe, or Bobby Orr.

That designation belongs to Darryl Sittler, who electrified the Toronto crowd with a 10-point effort that has stood for more than three decades.

Maple Leafs coach Red Kelly had revamped his lines a week before the game, putting a slumping Sittler between talented wingers Errol Thompson and Lanny MacDonald. It helped Toronto's cause that Boston was going with backup goaltender Dave Reece in what was to be his last start before returning to the minors.

Reece probably wished he had gone back a few days early.

Sittler's first point came on MacDonald's goal 6:19 into the first. Ian Turnbull made it 2–0—with Sittler registering another assist—at 16:54. Sittler's struggles appeared to be over.

He burst out the gate in the second, scoring three goals and adding a pair of assists for a seven-point night. The Leafs led 8–4, and Sittler was on the verge of something special.

"I didn't even know what the record was," admitted Sittler. "Our statistician came over after the second period and told me. That was the first I had even known there was a record. But going into the third period, the fans knew something was up."

His fourth goal of the game 44 seconds in the third period equalled the mark set by Canadiens legend "Rocket" Richard in 1944. With every ensuing Sittler shift, an excited buzz floated through the arena. Midway through the period, Sittler snagged the puck inside the Bruins zone and fired a long shot, which handcuffed Reece, giving Sittler the record by himself.

Sittler added a sixth goal—and tenth point—before the night was done, giving the hometown fans one more reason to celebrate. Sittler's astounding performance left him with a record not even Gretzky or Lemieux could touch.

"To pass Richard, a guy I've always admired and looked up to, was particularly special," said Sittler. "I'm proud to have held the record as long as I have."

39

Getty Images

BLUE JAYS CAPTURE FIRST AL EAST TITLE (1985)

TORONTO BLUE JAYS FANS must have believed the franchise was due—the players certainly did.

After languishing at the bottom of the standings for its first five years of existence, the team began steadily climbing the standings, finally capturing its first division title in 1985. The pennant victory served as the catalyst for a nine-year run of success that vaulted the franchise into baseball's elite.

After opening the 1985 season at an uninspiring 7–7, highlighted by an 8–7 loss to Baltimore in a game Toronto led 7–2, the Blue Jays went on an impressive tear, going 29–9 over their next 38 games. The run included winning streaks of five, seven, and eight games, and put the Jays up by seven and a half games over the second-place Tigers. At the all-star break, Toronto boasted a 53–35 record.

The Blue Jays continued their winning ways, going 13–2 over one stretch in late July to build a nine-and-a-half game lead in the AL East. It appeared that the Jays would cruise to their first-ever division title. However, the New York Yankees had other ideas, and a hot August helped the Bronx Bombers reduce Toronto's lead to a game and a half.

The Jays would build a sizable lead once more, only to have the Yankees close in again. Holding a magic number of two heading into their season-ending series at Exhibition Stadium, Toronto needed just one win to finish off the pesky Yanks once and for all. They got that victory courtesy of former New York hurler Doyle Alexander, who threw a complete-game five hitter in the pennant-clinching 5–1 triumph.

As outfielder George Bell snagged the final out, the Blue Jays flooded out of the dugout while more than 44,000 fans at Exhibition Stadium went crazy. With the victory, the Jays were no longer an expansion team. They were champions.

"When I was hugging Garth [Iorg] and [Jim] Clancy down on the field, I was saying, 'We made it through a long time and we made it through together,'" said Jays catcher Ernie Whitt, one of three original players still with the team.

"It's just an extra-good feeling" (The Canadian Press, October 5, 1985).

38

CANADIENS COMPLETE CUP FIVE-PEAT (1960)

WHEN IT CAME TO dynasties in the Original Six era, no team had a more dominant run than the Montreal Canadiens of the late 1950s.

By the time the 1959–1960 season had arrived, the Canadiens had already established one of the most incredible runs in professional sports history. And with their fifth consecutive Stanley Cup championship in 1960, the Canadiens concluded a period of NHL greatness that has never been matched.

There were signs that 1959–1960 would be the end of an era. Team captain Maurice "Rocket" Richard, a man who had meant so much to the Canadiens for so long, was now an injury-prone, out-of-shape 38-year-old whose best days on the ice were clearly behind him. There were questions about how much Richard would be able to contribute to another Stanley Cup quest.

Fortunately, Richard had plenty of talented teammates to pick up the slack.

The Canadiens rolled to a 40–18–12 record, finishing 13 points clear of the runner-up Toronto Maple Leafs. A trio of 30-goal scorers (Jean Beliveau, Henri Richard, and Bernie Geoffrion) led the offensive attack, while Richard added 19 goals despite missing 19 games with various injuries. Jacques Plante led all netminders in wins (40) and goals-against average (2.54) to win his fifth straight Vezina Trophy as the league's top netminder.

The Canadiens faced Chicago in the first round, having gone 7–3–4 against the rapidly improving Blackhawks during the regular season. The dominance continued in the post-season as Montreal rolled over the 'Hawks in four games. Chicago forward Bobby Hull, who led the league with 81 points, was held to a single goal in the whitewash.

That left the Toronto Maple Leafs as the last line of defence between Montreal and a fifth straight title. Yet, having battled to a six-game win over Detroit in round one, the Leafs had nothing left for the Habs, bowing out in four straight while scoring just five goals in the series.

Richard would hoist the Cup for the final time before retiring the following September, leaving the game as the leader of one of pro sports' most incredible teams.

The Canadian Press/COC

SANDRA SCHMIRLER FOURSOME NABS OLYMPIC GOLD (1998)

CHEERED ON BY her youngest fan, Sandra Schmirler was good as gold in Nagano.

Schmirler and teammates Jan Betker, Marcia Gudereit, Joan McCusker, and Atina Ford became the first women's team to ever win gold at the Winter Olympics. The victory wasn't without its nervous moments, including one that had the team believing it was out of the running for a gold medal.

Just two months after the birth of daughter Sara, Schmirler won an emotional Olympic trial in Brandon, Man., beating Shannon Kleibrink of Alberta 9–6 to advance to the Games.

"I don't think there's any greater prize than representing your country at the Olympics," said McCusker. "It's the chance of a lifetime. And we were fortunate enough to make it."

Canada opened the Olympics with a nerve-wracking 7–6 win over the U.S. before losing a 6–5 extra-end decision to the Norwegians. Facing intense scrutiny from the fickle Canadian media, the quartet proceeded to run the table, beating Japan, Denmark, Britain, Sweden, and Germany in succession to finish atop the round-robin with a 6–1 record.

Canada battled Britain in a semifinal match that went down to an extra end. Facing two British stones, Schmirler tossed her final rock, then watched in horror as it barrelled down the ice. She yelled "Oh, no!" as the stone stopped just in time. The single point gave Canada the win, and a spot in the gold-medal game.

"I was so fooled by that rock," McCusker said with a laugh. "I didn't want to believe it was heavy, but I couldn't believe it wasn't slowing down. Honestly, I thought we had lost."

Denmark awaited the Canadians in the final, and found itself playing catch-up the entire game. Schmirler counted three in the first end, led 5–2 at the fifth-end break, and ran the Danes out of rocks in the tenth end of a 7–5 victory.

The players tearfully received their gold medals and belted out "O Canada" at the top of their lungs. Between her new daughter and her Olympic medal, "Schmirler the Curler" was as happy as could be.

The Canadian Press/COC

FERGUSON JENKINS JOINS BASEBALL HALL OF FAME (1991)

FERGUSON JENKINS was a man of firsts.

After making headlines as the first Canadian pitcher to make a major-league all-star team, then becoming the first to capture the Cy Young Award, Jenkins completed the history-making trifecta in 1991, becoming Canada's first inductee into the Baseball Hall of Fame. Jenkins was remembered as one of the more durable pitchers of his era, finishing with 284 career wins.

Originally drafted by the Philadelphia Phillies, the native of Chatham, Ont., enjoyed an impressive run beginning with the Chicago Cubs in 1967. He registered six straight 20-win seasons, including a 24–13 mark in 1971, which earned him the Cy Young Award.

After two more seasons with the Cubs, Jenkins was dealt to the Texas Rangers in October 1973, where he went 25–12 the following season. The remarkable season earned him the Lou Marsh Trophy as Canada's Athlete of the Year.

Following a short stint in Boston and a return to Texas, Jenkins spent the final two years of his career with the Cubs, retiring in the place where he first established himself as one of the best hurlers of his generation.

Jenkins was passed over for Cooperstown in his first two years of eligibility. On his third try, he finally earned the required 75 percent of the ballot and joined Rod Carew, Gaylord Perry, Bill Veeck, and Tony Lazzeri in the Class of 1991.

Between his place in baseball's Hall of Fame, having a star on Canada's Walk of Fame, and being named to the Order of Canada, Jenkins knows he has plenty to be happy about.

"You're always happy when your country recognizes you for your accomplishments," said Jenkins. "Nothing comes easy in sports, and you don't ever do it alone. I had great teammates from four different organizations, and they all helped me become a better player."

"I was always in good shape right from spring training," said Jenkins. "That, combined with God-given ability, gave me the opportunity to face the challenge of completing ballgames, and being effective each and every game."

The Canadian Press/Frank Gunn

WOMEN'S HOCKEY STRIKES OLYMPIC GOLD (2002)

THE MEN GRABBED all the headlines, but they weren't the only ones to go home with Olympic hockey gold.

The Canadian women also left Salt Lake City as champions, gutting out a 3–2 win over the host Americans in a thrilling final between the sport's top teams. Making the win even sweeter was the fact that Canada had lost its last eight games against its North American rivals.

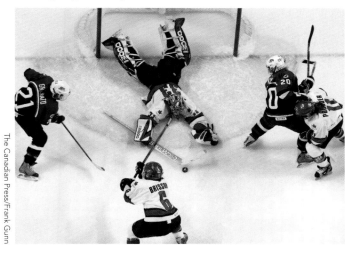

Though many believed the round-robin portion of the tournament would amount to little more than a glorified practice session for the tournament co-favourites, Canadian coach Melody Davidson wasn't about to take the rest of the field lightly.

"I don't feel that's ever an issue with our program," said Davidson. "We've always had a tremendous amount of respect for other teams."

Canada opened predictably strong, trouncing Kazakhstan 7–0. The Canadians followed with two more shutout wins, a 7–0 triumph over Russia and an 11–0 rout of Sweden.

The Americans had an equally easy time in their pool, scoring 27 goals while allowing just one. Their semifinal game, a 4–0 win over the Swedes, was much easier than

Canada's 7–3 victory over Finland. The Canadians actually trailed 3–2 after two periods before exploding for five goals in the third.

Danielle Ouelette gave Canada the lead less than two minutes into the gold-medal showdown, but U.S. forward Katie King tied the score early in the second. Hayley Wickenheiser restored Canada's lead shortly after, and Jayna Hefford made it 3–1 with just one second left in the period.

Karyn Bye closed the gap to 3–2 late in the third, but the Americans would get no closer. As the horn sounded, the Canadians swarmed goaltender Kim St.-Pierre, celebrating the biggest win of their careers.

"I don't think I really understood the impact of the win until I got back to Canada," Davidson said. "I was completely caught off guard by what it meant to women from all over the country.

"It's become so much more special as time has gone on, knowing we were a part of history."

JACKIE ROBINSON MAKES HISTORY WITH MONTREAL ROYALS (1946)

APRIL 18, 1946, will forever be known as a day that changed professional baseball and the people who were allowed to play it.

It was on that day that Jackie Robinson made his debut for the Montreal Royals, making him the first black man to appear in a triple-A minor-league game. Robinson would rewrite major-league history the following season, beginning a successful career with the Brooklyn Dodgers. But it was his summer with the Royals, beginning with that historic April appearance, which would first prove without a doubt that minority players belonged among the world's best.

Robinson made his Royals debut in Jersey City, N.J., with Roosevelt Stadium packed to the brim with more than 25,000 curious spectators. The newcomer didn't disappoint, pounding out a three-run homer and finishing with four hits and two stolen bases as Montreal walloped the New York Giants 14–1.

more tolerant of blacks than most U.S. communities, particularly those with baseball franchises.

As more than 16,000 fans crammed into Delormier Stadium for the Royals' home opener, Robinson was given the biggest ovation of any Montreal player. Robinson acknowledged the positive reaction, one of many he would receive during his one season in Canada.

Robinson would go on to star in his lone triple-A campaign, leading the league with a .349 batting average and .985 fielding percentage. The next season, Robinson began a Hall of Fame career with the Dodgers, smashing the colour barrier to pieces in one of the most transcendental events in sports history.

Many, including Robinson, doubt it ever would have happened had it not been for the city of Montreal, which welcomed the star second baseman into the community with open arms and an attitude of tolerance that simply didn't exist in his native country.

The biggest surge of support for Robinson came from Montreal baseball fans who largely welcomed the groundbreaking infielder into their city. The metropolis was by no means racism free, but it was considered far

The Canadian Press/COC

DANIEL IGALI GRAPPLES FOR GOLD (2000)

DANIEL IGALI IS no stranger to uphill battles.

The Nigerian-born wrestler faced his share of adversity prior to arriving in Victoria, B.C., in 1994 for the Commonwealth Games. After choosing to remain in Canada following the Games, Igali initially struggled with adjusting to his new home.

Igali earned his education, honing his wrestling skills, and did Canada proud, capping his inspiring story by winning the first-ever gold medal in wrestling for his adopted homeland.

"I was very glad that I was doing this for Canada," Igali said after returning home from Sydney. "I couldn't have done it for any other country. The Olympics is something I had in my head from when I was about 10 years old and it's now a dream that I've realized" (The Canadian Press, October 3, 2000).

Though Daniel thrived at B.C.'s Simon Fraser University, he still had his share of struggles. Having to work two jobs to keep his head above water, Igali often missed wrestling practice, which irked coach Dave McKay. A crushing loss at a 1996 tournament made Igali realize something needed to change.

With a renewed commitment to his training regimen, Igali became a force in Canadian wrestling, earning a fourth-place finish at the 1998 world championships. The following year, with adopted "mother" Maureen Matheny battling cancer, Igali captured gold at the worlds, qualifying for the 2000 Olympics. Just days after returning to Canada, Matheny passed away.

Igali was at his best in Sydney, cruising through his first three matches. Facing American Lincoln McIlravy in the semis, Igali clinched the victory with a stunning three-point throw in overtime.

That set up a gold-medal showdown with Russia's Arsen Gitinov. Igali burst out to a 4–0 lead, only to see Gitinov tie the score by the end of the first round. Igali regained the lead with a two-point manoeuvre, and added a third point by exposing Gitinov's back to the mat. That was all Igali needed in a 7–4 win.

Igali wept as "O Canada" played. After shedding tears of frustration and sadness so many times before, Igali was finally revelling in tears of joy.

The Canadian Press/COC

32

The Canadian Press

RICK HANSEN: MAN IN MOTION (1985–1987)

AS A TEENAGER, Rick Hansen dreamed of traversing the planet.

Years later, Hansen's wish came true and, thanks to his efforts, thousands of others have had their dreams realized as well.

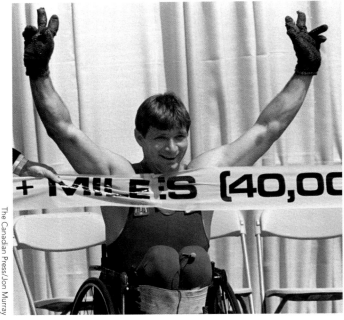

The Canadian Press/Jon Murray

Hansen, who was paralyzed from the waist down in a 1973 auto accident, spearheaded a crusade to cross the earth in a wheelchair to raise money for spinal cord research. More than two years later, he had amassed over 40,000 kilometres in 34 countries, raising $26 million for his cause while becoming a hero to Canadians in every province and territory.

Several factors went into Hansen's decision to hit the streets. As a 14-year-old, Hansen fantasized about cycling around the globe with friends. That desire was later coupled with inspiration and encouragement drawn from family and friends, who largely supported Hansen despite some initial apprehension.

"I honestly wasn't ready until I reached a point where I had been inspired and impacted by so many people in my life," says Hansen. "There were moments of self-doubt along the way, but I knew I had to seize the window of opportunity I had."

Hansen departed Vancouver on March 21, 1985, armed with a 6-metre motorhome and six of his closest friends. While Hansen savoured countless life-altering experiences, including a jaunt atop the Great Wall of China and a meeting with Pope John Paul II, donations poured in from all over.

Hansen returned to Canada on August 25, 1986, arriving in Cape Spear, Nfld., to a thunderous ovation. Nearly 10 months later, he wheeled into B.C. Place Stadium in Vancouver, two years, two weeks, and two days after beginning the tour. Hansen wanted to show the world that disabled people could still lead normal lives. What he proved was that they are also capable of orchestrating the extraordinary.

"I don't see myself as anything special, but I do feel connected," says Hansen. "When someone acknowledges me, it makes me realize how proud I am to be Canadian and to know I've had a unique opportunity to get to know Canada and Canadians through the Tour."

The Canadian Press/Globe and Mail

The Associated Press/Robert F. Bukaty

SIMON WHITFIELD WINS OLYMPIC TRIATHLON (2000)

SIMON WHITFIELD SHOULD HAVE panicked when a multi-bicycle accident sent him careening to the asphalt at the inaugural Olympic triathlon.

Instead, the Kingston, Ont., native kept his cool, ran like the wind, and captured one of Canada's most stunning Olympic gold medals.

The Associated Press/David Guttenfelder

"Unbelievable," Whitfield said shortly after his victory. "I've dreamed of this my entire life. I can't tell you how proud I am to be Canadian" (The Canadian Press, September 17, 2000).

Whitfield struggled with the 1.5-kilometre swim, emerging from the water in twenty-eighth place, nearly 40 seconds behind the leader. Whitfield was one of the world's best in both the 40-kilometre bike leg and the 10-kilometre run, but with so many strong competitors in front of him, a podium finish seemed next to impossible.

It didn't take long for those odds to improve dramatically. Whitfield exploded past competitors in the early stages of the bike competition, eventually rocketing into the top 10, just nine seconds off the lead.

All progress was lost soon after when Whitfield found himself in the middle of a twisted mess of bikes that claimed a dozen other riders. By the time he remounted, he had dropped back to twenty-fourth place.

"I crashed right into an American, just screamed a little bit, got back on my bike, chased my way back up," Whitfield said. "Then I got behind another crash. I just kept my head" (The Canadian Press, September 17, 2000).

Whitfield held out hope: his legs still felt fresh, and the run was his strongest event. He quickly passed one adversary after another, maintaining the fastest pace of the race. In the blink of an eye, he had rocketed up the standings, eventually seizing the lead from Stephan Vuckovic.

The German would quickly reclaim top spot, and the two duelled over the final few kilometres until Whitfield found one final burst. He surged past Vuckovic and crossed the line more than 13 seconds ahead of his weary opponent.

Whitfield cried on the podium, the gravity of the moment finally setting in. This was the first triathlon gold medal ever handed out at the Olympics, and it was all his.

BARBARA ANN SCOTT BECOMES SKATING QUEEN (1948)

A NEW CAR NEARLY COST Canada its first-ever Olympic figure-skating gold.

The city of Ottawa presented Barbara Ann Scott, dubbed "Canada's Sweetheart," with two sets of keys for her wildly successful 1947 season. Scott was given the keys to the city, and a set that belonged to a brand-new convertible. What 18-year-old could turn down the offer of a free automobile?

But Scott had to pass. The car represented a gift, and any amateur figure skater accepting such tokens would lose his or her status, resulting in disqualification from the Olympics. Scott desperately wanted a gold medal, and the following year, she got it.

Scott enjoyed the first of her many titles in 1940, capturing the Canadian junior championship as an 11-year-old. After winning her first senior title in 1944, Scott executed a rare double the following year, repeating as Canadian champion while capturing the North American crown as well. The difficult double earned Scott the 1945 Lou Marsh Award as the country's top athlete.

She defended her Canadian title again in 1946 before seeing her career skyrocket. In addition to winning the North American title for a second time, Scott became the first Canadian to ever win the European figure-skating championship in the event's 50-year history. She went on to capture the world championship in Stockholm, earning a second Lou Marsh Trophy and prompting the city of Ottawa to offer her a four-wheeled gift upon her return home.

No car was no problem for Scott, who would save her most extraordinary performances for the 1948 season. Scott skated a masterful figures program, winning gold at the Olympics in St. Moritz, Switzerland, despite having to deal with terrible ice and planes roaring overhead.

Scott would cap her dream season with Canadian, European, and world titles, picking up her third Lou Marsh Trophy. She returned to Ottawa, greeted by thousands of delirious fans. Noting her intention to become a professional, the city again offered her a convertible as a celebration of her incredible amateur career.

This time, she happily accepted.

The Canadian Press/Montreal Star/Peter Brosseau

MONTREAL EXPOS MAKE MAJOR-LEAGUE DEBUT (1969)

CANADA'S FIRST FORAY into major-league baseball featured plenty of low points, but oh, what a scintillating start.

The Montreal Expos made a splash unlike any expansion team before them, winning their regular-season and home-field debuts and adding a no-hitter, all in a 10-day span. While they finished with just 52 victories, the Expos earned a special place in sports annals, giving Canadians a professional sports team they could root for together.

"I remember looking over to my broadcast partner Russ Taylor, and seeing tears streaming down his face before that first game," said longtime Expos broadcaster Dave Van Horne. "That's when I first realized just how much having this franchise meant to everyone."

Jim "Mudcat" Grant started Montreal's first game, April 8, 1969, against Tom Seaver and the New York Mets. After the Expos staked Grant to an early 2–0 lead, the Mets stormed back with three runs in the bottom of the second, ending his day after 1 1/3 innings.

The Expos tied it up in the third inning and seized the lead in the fourth on the first home run in franchise history. Relief pitcher Dan McGinn, in just his third major-league at-bat, belted a solo shot off Seaver for what would be the only homer of his five-year career. Montreal later broke the game open with a four-run inning and held on for an 11–10 win.

Six days later, the team returned home for a series against the St. Louis Cardinals. McGinn was again the hero, breaking a 7–7 tie with a run-scoring single in the seventh inning. Mack Jones added five RBIs for the Expos.

Bill Stoneman would send fans into a tizzy three days later, tossing the first no-hitter in franchise history. Most major-league teams go decades between no-nos; the Expos had their first just nine games into their existence.

It barely mattered that Montreal would go on to lose 110 games and finish 48 games behind the division-champion Mets. The Expos had provided countless memorable moments in their inaugural season—and that was only the beginning.

The Canadian Press/Montreal Gazette

The Canadian Press/Andre Pichette

DENNIS MARTINEZ MAKES MONTREAL PERFECTION (1991)

"EL PRESIDENTE, EL PERFECTO!"

As Dave Van Horne uttered those four words on July 28, 1991, Montreal Expos pitcher Dennis Martinez entered baseball's elite, finishing off the thirteenth perfect game in major-league history and the first ever by a member of a Canadian-based team. The 27-up, 27-down masterpiece earned the native of Granada, Nicaragua, a special place in Canadian baseball history.

"It stands out, obviously, as one of the great moments in Expos history," said Van Horne. "And knowing Dennis, and how he turned his life and career around and enjoyed a second chance with the Expos, to be able to share the moment with him was very moving."

Martinez cruised through the first three innings, striking out three while inducing six ground-ball outs, a sign his sinking fastball was working. The Dodgers couldn't even get a ball out of the infield until Lenny Harris flied out to end the fifth.

"I remember very early in the game," Van Horne recalled, "maybe the third or fourth inning, [broadcast partner] Ken Singleton turned to me and said, 'I think we're in for something really special today. I've never seen Dennis so precise with all of his pitches.'"

After mowing down the Dodgers in the sixth, Martinez finally received some run support the next inning courtesy of two Alfredo Griffin errors that led to a pair of unearned runs for the Expos. Armed with a 2–0 lead, Martinez sent down the next six Dodgers in order, taking his perfect game to the ninth.

With the 45,560 at Dodger Stadium on their feet, Martinez induced Chris Gwynn to fly out to centre fielder Marquis Grissom for the final out, then burst into tears as his teammates converged on the mound. On a tidy 96 pitches, Martinez had achieved pitching perfection.

"Dodger Stadium is a ballpark rich in baseball history," said Van Horne. "Dodger fans have seen their share of great pitchers, from Sandy Koufax to Don Drysdale, and later Don Sutton.

"For Dennis to pitch a masterpiece of a game in that setting just made it all the more incredible."

The Associated Press/Craig Fujii

27

HOME SIDE WINS INAUGURAL CANADA CUP (1976)

FOUR YEARS AFTER beating Russia in the most legendary series in hockey history, Canada challenged the world—and won.

The Canadian Press

Six of the world's best hockey nations gathered for the inaugural Canada Cup, widely considered the greatest international competition to date. And just as they had done in 1972, the Canadians came out on top, fending off a pesky Czechoslovakian team in the final.

With 16 future Hall of Famers in the lineup, many consider the 1976 edition the greatest Canadian team in international hockey history.

"I went into the event in awe," said defenceman Larry Robinson. "As far as veteran leadership and experience goes, the '76 team has to rate as one of the best."

Canada opened with convincing wins over Finland, the U.S., and Sweden before getting doused with a splash of reality. Two days after the Sweden triumph, Canada ran into Czech goaltender Vladimir Dzurilla, who stonewalled the Canadians on the way to a stunning 1–0 win.

Undaunted, Canada ended the round-robin with a 3–1 victory over the U.S.S.R., setting up a best-of-three final against the defending world champions from Czechoslovakia, led by the towering Dzurilla.

"Dzurilla was so damned big, you can't see much of the net to start with," said Robinson. "But we knew we had too much talent. Somewhere down the line, we would find the weakness in his armour."

Dzurilla wasn't fooling anyone in Game 1, allowing four goals in the first period before giving way to backup Jiri Holocek. Canada cruised to a 6–0 victory that left many wondering if the final was destined to be a laugher.

The Canadians opened Game 2 with two quick goals, chasing Holocek from the net. This time, Dzurilla kept his country in the game long enough to force overtime with the score tied 4–4.

Dzurilla's magic ran out in the extra period. Canada's Darryl Sittler faked Dzurilla to the ice, then skated around the fallen netminder and deposited the game-winner, giving Canada the championship while preserving the country's hockey supremacy at the expense of not one, but five fallen foes.

The Canadian Press/Chuck Stoody

NORTHERN DANCER DAZZLES IN U.S. (1964)

NORTHERN DANCER'S LEGACY is twofold.

The Canadian thoroughbred has the distinction of being the most successful sire in North American history, producing 146 stakes winners across the globe. And his racing career was equally as impressive: Northern Dancer stunned the horse-racing world in 1964, winning a flurry of races, including two jewels of the U.S. Triple Crown, on the way to becoming the first horse ever inducted into the Canadian Sports Hall of Fame.

Northern Dancer won his first race in August 1963 and followed that up with a convincing victory in the Summer Stakes three weeks later. Later in the year, he reeled off five consecutive victories to earn Canadian Champion honours in the two-year-old colt category.

The following season, Northern Dancer went into the Bluegrass Stakes on a high after opening the season with two straight wins. Legendary jockey Bill Shoemaker had to choose between Northern Dancer and Hill Rise, Shoemaker's other regular ride. Shoe chose Hill Rise, believing he had a better chance at victory. Bill Hartack happily settled for Northern Dancer, leading the spurned horse to a half-length win at the Bluegrass.

The two horses met at the Kentucky Derby nine days later, Northern Dancer earned a neck victory, crossing the line in a track-record two minutes flat, a time bettered only by Triple Crown winner Secretariat in 1973.

The two went head to head once more at the Preakness, where Northern Dancer captured the second jewel of the Triple Crown by two lengths. A third-place finish in the Belmont Stakes ended his dream of becoming the first Canadian horse to win the American Triple Crown, but the three-year-old returned to form at the Queen's Plate in Toronto that June, cruising to a seven-length victory.

A tendon injury would cut short Northern Dancer's racing career, and he went on to stud the largest collection of race winners in thoroughbred-racing history. The horse

became one of the biggest names in his sport, something not even the great Bill Shoemaker saw coming.

WAYNE GRETZKY'S 215-POINT MASTERPIECE (1986)

BY THE TIME the 1985–1986 season rolled around, there wasn't much Wayne Gretzky hadn't accomplished.

He already owned the single-season records in goals, assists, points, short-handed goals, and hat tricks. His Edmonton Oilers had won back-to-back Stanley Cups. And he wouldn't turn 25 until the following January.

Still, Gretzky couldn't resist one more charge at the record books. And in his seventh season, he established one of the most unreachable benchmarks in sports, highlighted by a whole lot of playmaking.

"You have to produce every night, no question," said Gretzky. "Obviously I was helped by the players around me, and I was lucky to be surrounded by such gifted offensive players like Jari Kurri, Mark Messier, Paul Coffey, and others.

"We played hard every game, and at the end of the day, it just added up."

Gretzky began the 1985–1986 season on a tear, recording 24 points in his first 10 games. At the 20-game mark, the Brantford, Ont., phenom had 15 goals and 30 assists, typically strong numbers from Gretzky.

Then, he *really* started sharing the wealth.

Beginning with three helpers in a November 30 win over Hartford, Gretzky enjoyed a 14-game stretch where he recorded 39 assists. He notched his hundredth assist of the season in the Oilers' fifty-second game, putting him on pace to shatter his old record of 135 set the previous season. He had a seven-assist game in an 8–2 Valentine's Day massacre of the Quebec Nordiques, and broke his old record with assist No. 136 against Pittsburgh three weeks later.

The only question that remained was how high Gretzky could go. The answer to that question came on the final night of the season, when Gretzky registered assist No. 163—and point No. 215—in a 3–2 win over Vancouver. Gretzky had not only re-established the single-season scoring record, he had done so with an unnatural reliance on the pass.

Gretzky later said both his assists and points records would be "hard to beat." Leave it to "The Great One" to make one of hockey's greatest understatements.

The Canadian Press/Jacques Boissinot

JACQUES VILLENEUVE WINS F1 TITLE (1997)

THE 1997 FORMULA ONE SEASON was an up-and-down campaign for Jacques Villeneuve and, fortunately for him, it finished on a high note.

In one of the most hotly contested showdowns in F1 history, the St.-Jean-sur-Richelieu, Que., native held off Michael Schumacher to join one of the most elite fraternities in open-wheel racing, pulling out the championship in the final race of the season.

The Canadian Press/Ryan Remiorz

Villeneuve's start to the season was a rough one: he captured the pole in Australia, but was knocked out of the race at the first turn. Villeneuve atoned for his mistake three weeks later, earning the victory at the Brazilian Grand Prix.

He followed two weeks later with a victory in Argentina, opening up a comfortable lead in the standings, but followed with DNFs in each of the next two races.

"We would have amazing races, and then we would follow with very bad races," said Villeneuve. "That was the dilemma we faced. The car was faster than anyone's, but it was very difficult to drive."

Just as Villeneuve had leapt back into contention with a win in Spain, he crashed out on the first lap of the Canadian Grand Prix. It was a particularly disappointing result for Villeneuve, who desperately wanted to win in his native province.

"I felt like a total idiot," said Villeneuve. "I made a beginner's mistake, and sadly it happened in Montreal."

Despite the slip-up, Villeneuve trailed Schumacher by just one point heading into the season finale. Villeneuve ran behind Schumacher for most of the race, but was steadily gaining ground. As he attempted to pass his German rival on Lap 48, Schumacher steered hard into Villeneuve, causing Schumacher's car to conk out.

Villeneuve's vehicle was slowed but intact, and he crossed the line in third to capture the drivers' title. The victory earned him countless accolades, including the Lou Marsh Award as Canadian Athlete of the Year.

"Even though I grew up in Europe, my home was always Canada," said Villeneuve. "To be recognized by my country for what I do, it was definitely very special."

The Associated Press/Denis Paquin

The Canadian Press/Boris Spremo

GEORGE CHUVALO GOES THE DISTANCE WITH ALI (1966)

MUHAMMAD ALI ADMINISTERED nearly 40 knockouts in his legendary boxing career, yet, despite his best efforts, he couldn't take down George Chuvalo.

The Canadian Press/Boris Spremo

The Toronto boxer entered the ring with the iconic heavyweight champion in a 1966 bout at Maple Leaf Gardens. While Chuvalo lost a unanimous decision in a fight many people considered one-sided, his refusal to back down prompted the flamboyant Ali to proclaim Chuvalo as one of his toughest opponents. Chuvalo could not have asked for a greater compliment.

Chuvalo's shot at the championship came about after Ali's original opponent, WBA champion Ernie Terrell, backed out of their highly anticipated bout. At 182 centimetres tall and chiselled, Chuvalo was an imposing figure, and while few expected the local favourite to last more than four rounds with Ali, Chuvalo believed otherwise.

Chuvalo's strategy was clear from the opening bell: stalk the champion and beat him to a pulp. That proved to be difficult as Ali used his lightning quickness to evade the majority of Chuvalo's punches. When the hometown hero did manage to get close to Ali, he pummelled the champion with a flurry of body blows, only to have Ali egging him on to punch harder. The middle rounds saw more of the same: Chuvalo chased, while Ali evaded.

By the thirteenth, Chuvalo was running on empty, exhausted from pursuing Ali around the ring. Ali smelled a knockout, and pounded Chuvalo relentlessly over the final three rounds, laying his hardest jabs and hooks on Chuvalo's battered face. As the end-of-round bell rang for the fifteenth and final time, a bloodied Chuvalo plodded to his corner, having remained on his feet for the entire bout.

As expected, Ali earned a decisive victory. But the post-fight buzz was directed at Chuvalo, whom Ali called "the toughest man I ever fought." No man had ever gone 15 rounds with the champion until now. And while the outcome wasn't what Chuvalo was looking for, it still earned him the respect of boxing fans worldwide—and from millions of proud Canadians.

The Canadian Press/Boris Spremo

CATRIONA LE MAY DOAN'S GOLDEN ENCORE (2002)

WHEN CANADA NEEDED a gold medal the most, Catriona Le May Doan delivered.

The fiery Saskatoon native with the infectious smile gave Canadians reason to cheer with a victory in the 500-metre short-track speed-skating event at the 2002 Winter Games in Salt Lake City. It was Le May Doan's second straight gold medal in the discipline she dominated for a half-decade, and provided Canadians with an overwhelming sense of relief following one of the worst stretches of misfortune in the country's storied Olympic history.

"Everything that was supposed to happen the first week didn't happen," said Le May Doan. "We knew that people back home were asking, 'What happened to Canada?'

"I'm not sure if the athletes were all that concerned, but the support staff definitely was."

Le May Doan skated a strong first run, crossing the line in 37.30 seconds, just eight one-hundredths off her latest world-record time. Despite the impressive performance, her lead was just four one-hundredths over Monique Garbrecht-Enfeldt of Germany, who was close enough to make Canadian fans sweat it out.

Le May Doan wouldn't break her record the following day, but she didn't have to. Her time of 37.45 earned her a narrow victory over Enfeldt, giving Canada its long-awaited first gold medal of the Games following several agonizing near-misses.

"To be honest, I was relieved when I realized I had won," said Le May Doan. "I was relieved that we had done it, relieved that the result was what it should have been, relieved that it was all over.

"Shortly after I won, someone said to me, 'Things are back as they should be. Now things will come together for the rest of the country.'"

Those words rang true. Thanks to a successful second week, Canada returned home with 17 medals, including seven gold. By the end of the Games, nobody dwelled on the disappointments of week one. There was too much celebrating to do, beginning with the Saskatchewan native whose emotional victory gave her country the boost it so desperately needed.

The Associated Press

FERGUSON JENKINS CAPTURES CY YOUNG AWARD (1971)

FERGUSON JENKINS WAS KNOWN for finishing what he started, and in 1971, the Chicago Cubs pitcher parlayed that reputation into one of the finest pitching seasons ever assembled by a Canadian hurler.

In his fifth full season with the Cubs, the Chatham, Ont., native posted a 24–13 record with a 2.77 earned-run average, 263 strikeouts, and 30 complete games. The combination of elusiveness and endurance earned Jenkins the Cy Young Award as the NL's top pitcher, making him the first Canadian to snag the honour.

"I was more than happy to receive the award," said Jenkins. "I knew what it meant, and it was great to be recognized in that way."

Jenkins was the Cubs' sole salvation in April, earning three of the team's eight wins in the month. He continued his mastery into May, improving to 8–2 on the strength of seven straight victories.

A sensational July put Jenkins at the top of the Cy Young list. Following a July 2 loss to the Pirates, the pride of Chicago's North Side won six straight decisions, going the distance in each of them while compiling a collective 1.50 ERA with 46 strikeouts and just three walks.

Jenkins reached a number of significant plateaus by season's end, picking up his twentieth win of the season August 20 against Houston and establishing a new career high with his twenty-third victory a month later against Philadelphia.

Though New York Mets hurler Tom Seaver finished with a lower ERA (1.76) and more strikeouts (289), Jenkins had more victories and complete games. Voters favoured Jenkins's win total and durability, and he earned 17 first-place votes to become the first Cubs player to win a Cy Young.

"You look at the pitchers in my era, they were all talented, and they were all winning 20 games," said Jenkins. "I knew if I was going to compete, I would have to stay healthy, and go to the post every fourth day and perform well."

Jenkins did just that, establishing a single-season benchmark few Canadian pitchers have approached.

The Associated Press/Lenny Ignelzi

The Canadian Press/COC/Ted Grant

ALEX BAUMANN STRIKES GOLD IN THE POOL (1984)

WHEN THE CANADIAN OLYMPIC Committee needed someone to spearhead an effort to improve Canada's performance at the Summer Olympics, they turned to one of the country's all-time greats.

Swimmer Alex Baumann seemed like the perfect choice to help Canada reach the podium, since he had plenty of expertise in that area. Baumann rose to international prominence in 1984 with a double-gold swimming performance in Los Angeles that ranks as one of the most dominant Olympic efforts in Canadian history.

Baumann's swimming career took off almost immediately. He arrived in Sudbury, Ont., from his native Czechoslovakia at the age of five and took up swimming shortly after. Baumann was a natural in the pool—by the time he was 17, the lanky young man with the chiselled good looks had accumulated 38 Canadian records and owned the world mark in the 200-metre Individual Medley (IM). He quickly became one of the darlings of Canadian sport.

The only thing keeping Baumann from making his mark south of the border was a serious shoulder injury that torpedoed his chance to swim for Indiana University. Baumann decided to return to Sudbury for rehabilitation, and sat out the 1982 world aquatic championships in Guayaquil, Ecuador. He set his sights instead on a strong performance at the Commonwealth Games in Brisbane, Australia, later that year.

Heading up a strong Canadian team that included fellow future Olympian Victor Davis, Baumann celebrated his return to full strength by blasting the field in the 200-metre IM. He lowered his world-record time to two minutes, 2.25 seconds while winning the race by more than three and a half seconds. He went on to post the same margin of victory in the 400-metre IM, giving him two of Canada's nine gold medals at the Commonwealth Games.

Baumann was set to enter the Games on a high following a win in the 400-metre IM at the 1983 World University Games before tragedy struck: his father died from medical-related complications, leaving Baumann devastated. He had dealt with loss before: two years earlier, his brother Roman had committed suicide. In both cases, Baumann turned to the water for therapy.

Baumann arrived in Los Angeles as the country's top medal hope in the pool, a burden made easier to bear by the absence of the boycotting Soviet Union. For his accomplishments prior to the Games, Baumann was named flagbearer for the opening ceremonies. Most athletes would have felt added pressure after being given such an immense responsibility—but not Baumann, who proudly carried the country's flag at both the 1982 Commonwealth Games and the 1983 University Games.

In both events, Baumann went on to win gold—and the 1984 Olympics would be no different.

On July 30, Baumann fashioned a performance for the ages in the 400-metre IM, finishing in four minutes, 17.41 seconds, breaking his own world-record time by over a tenth of a second. Baumann's gold was Canada's first in the pool in 72 years.

He wasn't finished, capturing the 200-metre IM five days later—also in world-record time—to lead Canada to a 10-medal performance in the pool. Baumann and Davis enjoyed an incredible Games, combining for five medals (three gold, two silver) and three new world records.

"I think there was a lot less pressure [in the second race], but I still was nervous," Baumann admitted. "I just had to tell myself that I'd already won a gold medal and that anything from here on in was a benefit" (The Canadian Press, August 4, 1984).

Baumann was named Male Athlete of the Year, earned induction into the Canadian Olympic Hall of Fame in 1985, and joined the Canadian Sports Hall of Fame in 1987.

Nearly 20 years later, Baumann was once again called upon to lead his country to greatness, and if Baumann's performance in Los Angeles is any indication, Canadians should anticipate plenty more trips to the podium.

The Canadian Press/COC/Ted Grant

The Canadian Press/COC/O. Bierwagon

GAETAN BOUCHER DOUBLES UP IN SPEED SKATING (1984)

SOME PEOPLE, EVEN THOSE in his own country, considered Gaetan Boucher one of the cockiest speed skaters of his generation.

After his performance at the 1984 Winter Olympics, the Charlesbourg, Que., native had every reason to be. Boucher blitzed the field in Sarajevo, Yugoslavia, winning a pair of gold medals—two more than Canada would capture four years later as the host nation.

The Canadian Press/Doug Ball

Boucher was not your typical wide-eyed teenager at the 1976 Winter Olympics in Innsbruck, Austria. The confident skater had only been a national team member for a year, but he believed he could reach the podium in his first Olympics—and he nearly did, placing sixth in the 1,000-metre race. Boucher was disappointed, but it was clear bigger things were on his horizon. Unfortunately for Boucher, it was an American rival who emerged as speed skating's next big thing. Eric Heiden took the sport by storm, and cruised past

Boucher at the 1979 world sprint championship. Heiden carried the momentum into the 1980 Winter Olympics in Lake Placid, N.Y., beating Boucher to win gold in the 1,000-metre event.

Heiden went on to win five gold medals at the Games, while Boucher settled for a lone silver—one of just four Canadian medals at the Games—despite breaking the existing Olympic record by well over a second. Boucher was great, but Heiden was simply better.

Fortunately for Boucher, Heiden decided to leave the sport on top, retiring at the age of 22. That opened the door for Boucher, though the Canadian skater struggled in successive world sprint championships as Russian skaters—all of whom had missed the 1980 Olympics due to a boycott—were emerging as serious threats on the world stage.

The Canadian Press/COC/O. Bierwagon

Despite the threat of Soviet dominance, Boucher strongly believed he was the world's best heading into

the 1984 Games. The retirement of Heiden immediately following the 1980 Olympics eliminated the Canadian's top competition, and Boucher realized the 1,000-metre championship was his for the taking.

"I knew I would win the 1,000-metre race," said Boucher, who served as the country's flagbearer for the opening ceremonies. "There was no doubt in my mind. I had won every 1,000-metre event heading into the Games, so there were no worries there."

In a highly entertaining 500-metre event, Boucher captured a bronze, finishing two-tenths of a second behind race winner Sergey Fokichev of Russia. Though Boucher was disappointed, he knew his two best distances—the 1,000- and 1,500-metre events—remained. And his confidence level remained high as he attempted to become Canada's first gold-medal winner since 1976. Boucher said following his runner-up finish to Heiden in 1980 that he would capture gold in 1984—Soviet participation or not. And true to his word, Boucher glided down the outdoor Zetra Ice Rink, finishing the race in one minute, 15.80 seconds, more than eight-tenths faster than another Russian skater, Sergei Khlebnikov.

With the weight of a nation off his shoulders, Boucher set his sights on a third medal in the 1,500-metre race. Dealing with the lingering effects of a cold, Boucher fought through it and, in another exciting finish, held off Khlebnikov for his second gold of the Olympics. Boucher finished with two golds and a bronze, capturing three of Canada's four medals at the Games.

Boucher would go on to compete at the 1988 Winter Olympics in Calgary, but did not reach the podium. It was a subdued end to Boucher's stellar career, but the Quebec skater was still treated to a lengthy standing ovation after completing his final Olympic race. Canada would be held without a gold medal in 1988, adding further significance to Boucher's accomplishments four years earlier in Yugoslavia.

"I felt so much pride to have accomplished something that's always just a dream for a lot of people," said Boucher, who took home the 1984 Lou Marsh Award while becoming the first athlete in Canadian history to win three medals at a single Winter Olympics. "I was proud to have accomplished it, but I was more proud to have believed all along that I could do it."

MONTREAL EXPOS WIN DIVISION TITLE (1981)

LABOUR DISRUPTIONS have played a part in the best and worst moments in Montreal Expos history.

While the 1994 impasse denied Montreal its best shot at a championship—the team was 74–40 at the time—a strike actually benefited the Expos in 1981, helping the team earn Canada's first division title. The post-season would end without a World Series berth, but the rest of the National League had been served notice—the up-and-coming Expos had arrived.

"They had a remarkable team that year," said long-time Expos play-by-play man Dave Van Horne. "Most of the players had come up together from the farm system. They arrived together as a team, and they stayed

together, and I think certainly by 1981, the players started to feel the pressure to win."

That pressure began building after the 1979 season, when the Expos posted a franchise-best 95–65 record to finish just two games behind the division-champion Pittsburgh Pirates. The team electrified the city of Montreal by remaining competitive all season long, while Gary Carter and Andre Dawson represented the first wave of young talent that would quickly become the Expos' trademark.

The 1980 Expos finished 90–72, a game behind Philadelphia in the National League East standings. Carter posted his first 100-RBI season, while Dawson added 87 RBIs of his own. Veteran outfielder Ron LeFlore led the league with a franchise-record 97 steals, while Montreal's next rookie phenom—fellow speedster Tim Raines—made his Expos debut. The core of the team had never been stronger, and big things were expected from the Expos entering 1981.

The team opened the season with a bang, winning 11 of its first 13 games, but wasn't able to maintain the pace, dropping 16 of its next 26 games stretch to fall out of the division lead. Though the Expos were having trouble hitting home runs, Raines was providing more than enough speed in place of LeFlore, who had departed for the Chicago White Sox as a free agent in the off-season. Raines batted .338 and had 40 steals through the first 39 games of the season—making him not only a contender for the Rookie of the Year award, but earning him whispers as a potential all-star in his first full year in the league.

With the Expos sitting at 30–25 on June 11, the Players' Association voted to strike, as owners and players failed to reach an agreement on the league's contentious free-agent policy. The labour disruption left the season—and Montreal's playoff chances—in peril.

Play resumed August 10, with the league splitting the season into two halves. The division winners from each half would face off in a best-of-five series, with the victor moving on to the league championship series. Suddenly, the Expos had something to play for again. Carter, Dawson and Raines were named to the National League all-star team, giving the trio an extra boost of confidence heading into the second half of the season.

The team began the "new" season with 11 wins in their first 17 games and, despite losing the lead in early September, they heated up again at the end of the month to seize a slim advantage. Expos fans had seen their team fall short in each of the past two seasons, and knew that one bad weekend to close the season would extend the team's post-season drought once more.

Montreal needed two wins against the New York Mets at Shea Stadium at season's end to clinch the division. The Expos opened the series with a 2–0 victory on the strength of a two-hit shutout from Steve Rogers, leaving them one victory shy of their long-awaited first post-season berth.

The next day, the Expos rallied from a three-run deficit and seized the lead in the seventh inning on a two-run triple from late-season call-up Wallace Johnson. Closer Jeff Reardon preserved the lead, retiring Dave Kingman on a fly ball to left for the final out, igniting pandemonium on the field and in the Montreal dugout.

After 12 long seasons, Canada's team was finally headed to the playoffs.

BIG BEN GALLOPS TO GOLD IN SEOUL (1988)

NO CANADIAN ATHLETE FELL as far as quickly as Ben Johnson.

The Jamaican-born sprinter betrayed millions of fans when he tested positive for steroids just three days after winning the 100-metre title at the 1988 Olympics in Seoul. Johnson quickly became a national disgrace, and his name still evokes anger and frustration from those who revelled when he destroyed the field in South Korea.

"For a Canadian to win one of the glamour events of the Summer Games, it was incredible," said longtime Olympic broadcaster Brian Williams. "This was such a significant event ... a great tragedy that overshadowed great performances by other Canadian athletes."

Johnson, who emigrated to Canada from Jamaica in 1975, first delighted hometown track fans with a pair of silver-medal performances at the 1982 Commonwealth Games in Australia. Known for his explosiveness out of the starting blocks, Johnson posted a time of 10.05 seconds in the individual final and added a second medal in the men's 4 x 100–metre relay.

Despite struggling at the 1983 world championships in Helsinki—crossing the line sixth in 10.44 seconds—Johnson was considered one of Canada's best shots at a podium finish at the 1984 Summer Olympics in Los Angeles. Johnson reached the final, where he captured bronze in 10.22 seconds. Johnson added a third-place finish in the relay, and finished the year with a Canadian-record run of 10.12 seconds.

Johnson's next goal was to beat American arch-nemesis Carl Lewis, who soundly trounced Johnson at the 1984 Olympics and was riding high as the best male sprinter on the planet. Johnson finally ousted Lewis in 1985 after losing to the speedster in seven consecutive competitions. Before long, Johnson and Lewis were engaged in track and field's most entertaining and engaging tête-à-tête—both men believed they were superior sprint-

ers, and as the rivalry grew, both runners' times improved dramatically.

After Johnson captured gold at both the 1986 Goodwill Games and the 1986 Commonwealth Games, it was clear the Canadian sprinter had an edge on his American counterpart. Johnson punctuated his newfound dominance

with a record-shattering victory at the 1987 world championship in Rome, crossing the line in 9.83 seconds—a full tenth faster than the previous mark held by Calvin Smith. The sensational season earned Johnson both the Associated Press Male Athlete of the Year award and the Lou Marsh Award as outstanding Canadian athlete.

Johnson's remarkable performances left a bitter taste in Lewis's mouth. After first contending that he was battling a debilitating stomach virus at the world championship, Lewis made an even more stunning revelation—he was certain that countless world-class sprinters were using performance-enhancing drugs. Johnson scoffed at the allegations, while others suggested Lewis was simply being a sore loser.

Johnson's 1998 campaign started on a sour note after he suffered a hamstring injury early in the season, one that hampered him until the summer. His first meeting of the season with Lewis resulted in a third-place finish, leading the cocky American to proclaim that the Olympic gold would be his.

On September 24, Lewis and Johnson lined up for the showdown the entire world had been waiting for. Canadians had seen Johnson dominate the 100-metre event for most of the previous two years, and they were expecting gold in Seoul.

Johnson rocketed out of the blocks, leaving the field a full stride behind. Lewis attempted to gain ground, but Johnson never slowed, raising his arm as he crossed the finish line in a world-best 9.79 seconds. Johnson quickly grabbed a Canadian flag, waving it proudly during his victory lap.

Canadians celebrated right along with him, staying up until the wee hours of the morning to catch the history-making race. Newspapers labelled it one of Canada's most poignant sporting moments. Having won Canada's first men's 100-metre medal since Harry Jerome in 1964 while improving his world record by four one-hundredths of a second, there was nothing left for Johnson to do in his career, nowhere left to go—except down.

That's exactly where he ended up after his subsequent urine sample revealed traces of steroids. The *Toronto Sun* summarized fans' feelings with a simple two-word headline: "Why, Ben?"

Decades later, those who remember the ecstasy of Johnson's victory and the agony of his subsequent demise are still asking that question.

The Associated Press

MAURICE RICHARD: FIRST TO 50 GOALS (1945)

THE NHL'S 50-goals-in-50-games club is one of the most elite in any sport. Just five players in the history of the game have reached the elusive plateau: Maurice Richard, Mike Bossy, Wayne Gretzky, Mario Lemieux, and Brett Hull.

The Canadian Press/Montreal Gazette

Gretzky reached 50 goals the fastest. He, Lemieux, and Hull even cracked the 80-goal plateau, but Richard's membership in the 50-in-50 club is easily the most impressive of all. That's because Richard scored his record-breaking fiftieth goal back in 1945, and for 35 seasons, he was the sole member of the 50-in-50 club, leading many to proclaim him the greatest goal-scorer in hockey history.

Richard's path to NHL greatness was fraught with setbacks. While playing for the Canadiens' farm team of the same name, the Montreal native suffered a pair of serious injuries—one to his wrist, the other to his ankle. Not only did the ailments keep him from reaching the big club, they also prevented him from enlisting in the army for World War II. Fans and coaches were concerned that perhaps Richard was too brittle for the physical NHL.

Richard showed flashes of brilliance in his first season with the Canadiens in 1942, scoring five goals and adding six assists in 15 games before a broken ankle ended his season just two days after Christmas. Once again, Canadiens fans were left wondering if their hometown hero would ever live up to the hype.

Their hopes were realized the very next season, when Richard erupted for 32 goals in just 46 games, making him the fourth player in league history to crack the 30-goal barrier. Richard saved his best work for the playoffs, scoring 12 times in just nine games as the Canadiens won their first Stanley Cup championship since 1931. Richard's doubters had been silenced, and die-hard supporters were left wondering exactly how good "The Rocket" could be.

For the second straight season, Richard was teamed with Elmer Lach at centre and Toe Blake on right wing, forming the legendary "Punch Line" that would torment opposing teams on a nightly basis. This was especially true on December 28, 1944, when Richard enjoyed the game of his life mere hours after lugging boxes, furniture, and even a piano into his new two-storey Montreal home. Richard exploded for an NHL-record eight points (five goals, three assists) in a 9–1 rout of the Detroit Red Wings, adding to Richard's rapidly growing legend.

Richard entered the February 25, 1945, game against the Toronto Maple Leafs with 44 goals, one shy of breaking Joe Malone's single-season record. Though the Leafs did everything in their power to shut down "The Rocket," Richard would not be denied, scoring with less than four minutes to go for his historic forty-fifth goal of the season.

With the single-season record in his possession, just one milestone remained, one that seemed untouchable: 50 goals. Richard entered the fiftieth game of the season against Boston needing one goal to get there. Like the Toronto game three weeks earlier, Richard was stymied over the first two and a half periods. But with just over two minutes left, Richard took a Lach pass and beat Boston netminder Harvey Bennett for the historic goal. Richard would finish with his first of four NHL goal-scoring titles, and was named to the league's all-star team for the second year in a row. Most significantly, a player once deemed too fragile for the NHL had broken one of the league's most impenetrable scoring marks. Richard not only belonged in the league, he was now its biggest star, and would remain that way for over a decade. And while four other legends have since joined Richard in the 50-goals-in-50-games fraternity, the mighty Montrealer will always be the original member.

The Canadian Press/Montreal La Presse

The Canadian Press/COC

PERCY WILLIAMS: DOUBLE GOLD IN AMSTERDAM (1928)

A LITTLE MAN from Vancouver ended up as one of Canada's biggest Olympic heroes.

Percy Williams was one of the smaller competitors at the 1928 Games in Amsterdam, weighing just 57 kilograms. But it was Williams's powerful motor that earned him international acclaim after the 20-year-old stunned audiences with victories in both the 100- and 200-metre races. Never before had a Canadian won the two most significant sprints in the same Olympic year, and no Canadian has done it since.

Williams overcame long odds to become a Canadian Olympic icon. He struggled with rheumatic fever throughout his childhood, an inflammatory disease which left him with a severely weakened heart. Doctors told him to avoid any strenuous activity, fearing his heart wouldn't be able to handle it.

Williams ignored the doctors' advice and took up sprinting, despite weighing no more than 56 kilograms for the majority of his track and field career. Williams showed an immediate proficiency in the shorter events, succeeding by conserving energy early in races before finding another gear as he approached the finish line. Observers were astonished at how fast Williams could run despite being so small—an accomplishment Williams owed completely to coach Bob Granger, who mentored Williams from the moment he began competing.

After dominating in high school and various international meets, the 1928 British Columbia Olympic trials provided Williams with the first chance to take his sprinting to another level. Williams not only bettered the field in the 100-metre event, he did so in a time of 10.6 seconds, equalling the Olympic record at the time.

Three weeks later, Williams travelled to Hamilton, Ont., where he won both the 100- and 200-metre national Olympic trials. The result was particularly satisfying for Williams, who had been dogged by critics from the outset of his racing career and was forced to overcome several hurdles along the way to a berth in the 1928 Olympics. It took a spirited canvassing effort from Williams's mother to raise enough money to send Granger to Amsterdam for the Games. His presence would prove to be worth every cent.

Despite the overwhelming victory back home, Williams entered the Games as an underdog. How would a shy 20-year-old, barely out of high school, fare with the eyes of the world upon him? It surprised many—both at the Games and back home—that Williams even qualified for the final. He certainly wasn't expected to reach the podium.

As Williams lined up at the start, he was dwarfed by his competitors, which included American favourite Robert McAllister, Great Britain's Jack London and George Lammers of Germany. Just under 11 seconds later, it was the Canadian busting the tape at the finish line, stunning the track and field community while winning the country's first Summer Games gold since the 1920 Games in Antwerp, Belgium.

After edging Charlie Borah of the U.S. by less than a metre in the 200-metre semifinal the next day Williams found himself matched up against young up-and-comer Helmut Kornig of Germany in the championship race. After allowing Kornig to set the pace for most of the race, Williams burst ahead in the final metres, shocking the world once more. Dutch fans rained cheers down on Williams, who had just orchestrated a most improbable double.

Williams took his show on the road following the Olympics, tearing through the U.S. on a tour that saw him lose just once in 22 races over a three-week period. He went on to break the world record at the 1930 Canadian championship in Toronto, crossing the line in 10.3 seconds to end Charley Paddock's nine-year reign as world record-holder. All this from a man who later admitted that he never really enjoyed running.

Williams left the sport behind him after retiring in 1932 due to a thigh injury. His career was short, but with two Olympic gold medals and dozens of other victories against world-class athletes, it was sensational.

The Canadian Press/COC

WAYNE GRETZKY REACHES 50 GOALS IN 39 GAMES (1981)

HOCKEY FANS HAD SEEN what Wayne Gretzky was capable of just two seasons into his legendary NHL career.

But not even the most ardent Gretzky supporter could have expected what "The Great One" accomplished in season No. 3.

The 20-year-old rocked the NHL record books, completing one of the game's most difficult tasks in absurd fashion. Only Maurice Richard and Mike Bossy had ever scored 50 goals in their team's first 50 games, and both reached the plateau in their final game. In 1981, Gretzky became the third member of the club with 11 games to spare.

"This one's probably my favourite individual record," said Gretzky. "One day someone will come along and beat it, but I think this one will ultimately be the hardest to break."

Though Gretzky built a reputation as the game's premier passer, his goal-scoring prowess was equally as impressive. As a 17-year-old, Gretzky scored 70 goals in 64 games for the Sault Ste. Marie Greyhounds of the Ontario Hockey League. A year later, he had 46 goals for the Indianapolis Racers and the Edmonton Oilers of the World Hockey Association.

Gretzky was considered the centrepiece of the Oilers' new National Hockey League franchise, though some questioned whether the rail-thin centre could succeed in the more rugged NHL. Gretzky put any doubts to rest early on, scoring 51 times and finishing with 137 points in his rookie season. The 19-year-old finished tied for the league lead in points with Los Angeles Kings legend Marcel Dionne, but lost the scoring title because Dionne finished with more goals.

Gretzky didn't need to worry about a tiebreaker the following season, pouring in an NHL-record 164 points (55 goals, 109 assists) to earn his first Art Ross Trophy as league scoring champion. At just 20 years old, Gretzky was the greatest player in the league—and was on the fast track to becoming one of the greatest players in history.

His third season left no doubt.

Gretzky opened the 1982–83 season by scoring in bunches. In a three-game span early in the season, Gretzky scored eight times, bringing his total to 15 in 14 games. Gretzky maintained a goal-per-game pace for the next two weeks before going on another scoring binge, tallying nine times in four games. A brief scoring drought gave way to another hot streak, leaving him with 40 goals in just 36 games.

After scoring a goal in Game 37, Gretzky led the Oilers against Los Angeles and Philadelphia to conclude a five-game late-December homestand. Gretzky abused the Kings, scoring four times in a 10–3 rout. Three nights later, the unsuspecting Flyers became the victims of one of Gretzky's greatest performances.

His first goal came on a five-foot tapper from the left of the crease. His second was a slapshot from between the face-off circles, and his third and fourth were from similar spots on the ice. And when the Flyers pulled goaltender Pete Peeters in favour of an extra attacker, Gretzky had the easiest of his 50 goals that season—a soft wrister into an empty net. With nine goals in two games, Gretzky owned hockey's most unattainable record: 50 goals in just 39 games.

"I never imagined getting 50 in 39, especially against Philadelphia," recalled Gretzky. "I was fortunate that night—everything just clicked."

Gretzky would go on to score 92 goals, shattering the previous record of 76 set by Phil Esposito 11 seasons earlier. The feat earned him his third consecutive Hart Memorial Trophy as NHL most valuable player, and he finished with 212 points—also a league record. More than 80 players have scored 50 goals in a season, but no one has done it more quickly than Wayne Gretzky—and it's possible that no one ever will.

The Canadian Press/Dave Buston

The Canadian Press/Paul Chiasson

CANADA COMES UP GOLDEN IN ATLANTA RELAY (1996)

ROBERT ESMIE'S HAIRCUT said it all.

The Sudbury, Ont., sprinter had the words "Blast Off" shaved into his hair prior to the men's 4 x 100–metre relay race at the 1996 Summer Olympics in Atlanta. The coif grabbed plenty of headlines in Canada, but was largely ignored in the U.S., where all eyes were on the heavily favoured hosts. Esmie, Bruny Surin, Glenroy Gilbert, Carlton Chambers, and Donovan Bailey were eager to crash the party, and when they blasted off on August 3, 1996, the Canadians put the Americans in their place, capturing gold in decisive fashion as the stunned crowd fell silent.

The Canadian Press/Andrew Vaughan

"As the leader of the team, my motivation was to tell guys that we were ranked number one in the world, and at no point in Olympic history had a relay team beat America," said Bailey. "We not only beat America, we crushed them in their own backyard."

Bailey's pre-race proclamation had been echoed by fans and analysts alike. The Americans simply didn't lose in the Olympic relay final: In 17 gold-medal races, the U.S. team won 14 gold medals and set 11 world records (they also failed to finish three times). The message going into the competition was simple: If the Americans completed the race, they would likely win it.

Bailey believed differently. The electrifying Canadian had barely caught his breath after winning the individual 100-metre title in world-record time when he expressed his desire to beat the powerhouse Americans on their own soil. Having already experienced the joy of standing atop an Olympic podium, Bailey wanted nothing more than to repeat the feat with four of his closest friends.

The Canadians looked slightly better than ordinary in qualifying, while the Americans blitzed their way through the heats, looking as strong as they ever had. American relay coach Charlie Green was certain the U.S. would win gold, and American media felt the same way. Bailey was having none of it—Canada was still the defending world champion in the relay, even if the title was won after the Americans were disqualified for dropping the baton.

Both teams faced injury concerns entering the gold-medal race. Chambers was replaced by Esmie as Canada's lead runner, and the team insisted it wouldn't miss a beat. American sprinter Leroy Burrell was also hurt, but his absence created far more controversy. Talk centred around whether nine-time gold medallist Carl Lewis would take Burrell's place on the team, despite not spending any time training with the relay squad. U.S. officials elected to leave Lewis off the team, leading to a media-driven distraction that may have played a role in the Americans' eventual undoing in the final.

In front of more than 83,000 fans at Centennial Olympic Stadium, the Canadians and Americans engaged in a memorable showdown. Lead runners Esmie and Jon Drummond were in a dead heat, but Canada had a smoother baton exchange and seized the early lead. U.S. second Tim Harden, subbing for the injured Burrell,

could only watch as Gilbert shot down the backstretch. Canada had the better baton pass again, and the lead grew even larger.

Surin, who failed to make the 100-metre final, atoned for his disappointment by extending the lead. When Surin handed the baton to Bailey, the race had already been decided. Bailey rocketed toward the finish, leaving Tim Montgomery a distant second, before coasting over the line in 37.69 seconds, just three-tenths of a second off the world record.

"It didn't matter whether we were ahead or behind at the time ... I just wanted the baton," said Bailey. "When I saw the final exchange, I knew it was over."

Had Bailey gone full out, the world record would have belonged to Canada—and Bailey even apologized to fans and teammates for easing up at the finish. But the Americans could keep their place in the record books. Canada had proven itself on the world's biggest stage, decimating the home team and ending the Americans' relay dominance.

The Associated Press/David Zalubowski

LARRY WALKER TAKES HOME NL MVP AWARD (1997)

LARRY WALKER WON'T SOON forget the 1997 season, and neither will stat-happy baseball fans.

Walker's incredible season will forever rank among the best of the twentieth century. The 31-year-old established career highs in home runs (49), RBIs (130), stolen bases (33), and batting average (.363) for the Colorado Rockies to become the first Canadian to ever win the National League's Most Valuable Player award.

The Associated Press/Gene J. Puskar

"It was just a pure, dominant offensive season," said Canadian Press baseball writer Shi Davidi. "The offensive numbers speak for themselves, and it's an accomplishment that every Canadian baseball player should want to try to mimic."

The baseball world was already well aware of Walker's offensive explosiveness. Walker enjoyed five productive seasons with the Montreal Expos, leading the team to baseball's best record in 1994 before a labour disruption ended the season prematurely. The Maple Ridge, B.C., native became a free agent following the season as the cash-strapped Expos watched their core players de-

part en masse. The Rockies came calling with a lucrative multi-year contract, and Walker suddenly found himself as one of the go-to sluggers in the best hitters' parks in the major leagues.

His first two seasons produced mixed results. After a 36-homer, 101-RBI season in 1995, Walker managed just 83 games in 1996 after suffering a broken clavicle. Though his power numbers were respectable (18 HR, 58 RBI), he batted just .276 after hitting over .300 in each of his previous two seasons. The regression at the plate, combined with Walker's inability to remain healthy over a full season, left fans pondering whether the personable outfielder would ever realize his full potential.

Walker's opening month was a sign of things to come: The right fielder batted .456 in April, with 11 homers and 29 RBIs in just 23 games. The barrage included a three-homer, five-RBI effort against the Expos, the team that signed Walker as an amateur in 1984.

Walker maintained a batting average above .400 through the end of June, with 25 home runs and 68 RBIs. He and his fans knew that if Walker could avoid both a lengthy slump and a trip to the disabled list, he would be given serious consideration for league MVP honours.

Walker remained in good health, and avoided any mid-season swoons. He bashed 24 homers over the final three months, and finished the season in the top-three in eight offensive categories. His steals ranked seventh in the league, and he added 11 outfield assists on the way to his third Gold Glove. At season's end, Walker earned 22 of a possible 28 first-place MVP votes to win in a romp over L.A. Dodgers catcher Mike Piazza.

He went on to finish second to Formula One champion Jacques Villeneuve in voting for the Lou Marsh Award as Canada's most outstanding athlete. The result irked Walker, who expressed incredulity at having "lost to a machine." He earned sweet redemption by winning the

1998 Lou Marsh Award despite finishing with lower numbers (23 HR, 67 RBI, .363 AVG.)

The 1997 season proved to be the highwater mark for Walker, though he did go on to enjoy two more 30-homer seasons and capture three National League batting titles during his tenure in Denver. Walker finished his career with a .313 batting average, 383 home runs and 1,311 RBIs while making five NL all-star teams and capturing seven Gold Glove awards. Walker's only regret? Not winning a championship, though he did reach the 2004 World Series, where his St. Louis Cardinals were swept by the Boston Red Sox. Walker later said he would have traded every award he has ever worn for a chance to win a World Series.

While he likely won't make the Hall of Fame, Walker is still considered the greatest player Canada has ever produced, a sentiment shared among fans and players alike.

"I've heard some good things from players coming up that I was an influence for them," said Walker. "You have no idea how much that means and how good a feeling that is."

The Associated Press/Dusan Vranic

CINDY KLASSEN DOMINATES WINTER OLYMPICS (2006)

THE CANADIAN OLYMPIC Committee boldly predicted its team would win 25 medals at the 2006 Winter Olympics in Turin, Italy. Considering the country's previous high was 17 medals in Salt Lake City four years earlier, the COC's expectations seemed unrealistic.

The Canadian Press/Paul Chiasson

Canada wound up just one medal shy of its projected total, and Cindy Klassen was the reason. The Winnipeg speed skater shot into the record books, winning five medals and becoming Canada's most decorated Olympian.

"My goal was just to do better than I had in the previous Olympics," said Klassen, who arrived in Italy with just one Olympic medal—a bronze—to her credit. "Anything over and above that would have been a bonus."

Like most kids who strap on the blades, speed skating wasn't Klassen's first choice. Though she took part in a number of different sports, hockey was far and away her favourite pastime right from the age of five. Klassen competed against boys at every level with the intention of playing for Canada at the 1998 Winter Olympics in Japan, the first Games to feature women's hockey.

Despite suiting up for the national junior women's team in 1996, Klassen was left off the Olympic roster. She was heartbroken, but vowed to continue working toward a possible spot on the 2002 Olympic team. While she was playing hockey for the University of Manitoba, her parents suggested she take up speed skating. Despite being reluctant at first, Klassen eventually relented—and a star was born.

By 1999, Klassen was already a member of the national junior team. She captured the 1,000-metre event at the world junior championships in Geithus, Norway, and added a third-place result in the 500-metre race. The following year, she joined the senior national team and continued her climb up the world rankings, earning three top-10 results at the 2001 world single distance championships. The decision to scrap hockey for speed skating was looking better by the year.

Klassen's first Olympic experience was a positive one. She placed third in the women's 3,000-metre competition at the 2002 Games in Salt Lake City, and added fourth-place finishes in the 1,500-metre and 5,000-metre races. Just as Klassen was reaching her peak, she suffered a horrible injury, severing 12 tendons in her arm after crashing into a group of skaters. Remarkably, she returned to the ice just a few months later, and won two medals at the 2004 world single distance championships.

Klassen reached the pinnacle of her sport in 2005, winning the overall 1,500-metre title. She headed to the 2006 Olympics as the world-record holder in the 1,500 and 3,000, and was considered Canada's best shot at a multi-medal performance. Klassen welcomed the challenge, though the goals she had set for herself were remarkably modest for an athlete expected to make at least two trips to the podium.

Surprisingly, things didn't start out so well for Klassen. A world-record holder in the 3,000-metre event, Klassen faded over the final two laps of the race and had to settle for bronze. Her fortunes brightened when she teamed with Kristina Groves, Christine Nesbit, and Clara

Hughes to capture silver in the team pursuit, and she saved enough energy to place second in the 1,000-metre event for her third medal of the Games.

Riding a wave of confidence, Klassen prepared for her biggest race of the Games—the 1,500-metre competition, where she also held the world standard. Klassen burst out to a fantastic start and maintained a speedy pace throughout, crossing the line with the fastest time of the competition. One pairing later, Klassen found herself atop the podium with her first Olympic gold medal.

Groves's second-place finish made the moment that much sweeter.

Klassen added a bronze medal—her fifth podium result of the Games—in the 5,000-metre race. The outstanding performance earned her flag-bearer honours at the closing ceremony, and she went on to win the 2006 Lou Marsh Award as Canadian Athlete of the Year.

"It was pretty neat," said Klassen. "The year couldn't have gone much better than it did. I'm very grateful and thankful to God for giving me the gift of speed skating."

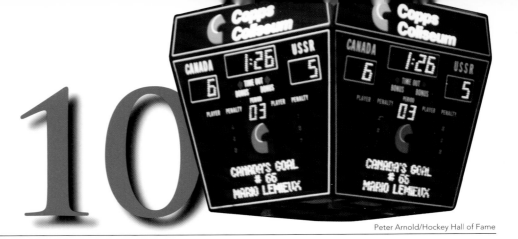

CANADA BEATS RUSSIA IN THRILLING CUP FINAL (1987)

ON THEIR OWN, both Wayne Gretzky and Mario Lemieux enjoyed their share of historic hockey moments.

Teamed together, hockey's ultimate dynamic duo put the finishing touches on a truly memorable performance. Lemieux's goal with 1:26 left in the third period gave the Canadians a 6–5 victory over the Soviet Union in the third and deciding game of the 1987 Canada Cup, widely considered the greatest hockey tournament ever played.

"This win cemented the fact that Canada was back now as the very best team in the world and had the best hockey players in the world," said longtime hockey writer Al Strachan. "Canada had played the style of game that the Russians had created, and we had beaten them at it.

"Canada's position at the top of the mountain had been re-established."

The host team was coming off a victory at the 1984 Canada Cup, but things didn't come easily. The Canadians stumbled to a fourth-place finish in the round-robin before knocking off the heavily favoured Soviets in overtime and sweeping Sweden in the best-of-three final. Knowing that the Soviets would be putting together their strongest team to date, Canada would need to be even stronger to repeat as champion.

From a talent standpoint, it would be hard to top the roster Canada put together. Gretzky and Lemieux were the two best players on the planet. They were joined up front by future Hall of Famers Mark Messier, Dale Hawerchuk, Doug Gilmour, and Michel Goulet. The defence was anchored by legends Ray Bourque and Paul Coffey, who would go on to become the highest-scoring blue-liners in NHL history. Grant Fuhr led the way in goal, joined by Ron Hextall and Kelly Hrudey.

The defending champions may have been a little overconfident at the outset of the tournament, and it nearly

led to a monumental upset. David Volek's power-play goal with 13 minutes left gave upstart Czechoslovakia a 4–4 tie with the Canadians in the opening game for both teams. The Czechs gave Canada all sorts of trouble—none more so than goaltender Dominik Hasek, who would go on to become a six-time Vezina Trophy winner in the NHL.

The Canadians rebounded with their strongest game of the round-robin, a 4–1 victory over Finland. Canada followed with a thrilling 3–2 victory over the U.S., on the strength of a Lemieux hat trick. A 5–3 win over Sweden earned the Canadians a spot in the semifinals even before concluding the round-robin against the Soviets. The teams duelled to a 3–3 draw in what was expected to be a championship preview.

Both teams did as expected in the semis, with Canada slipping past the plucky Czechs 5-3. After falling behind 2-0 through one period, Lemieux had two of Canada's three goals in a 2:25 span of the second period to give the home team the lead for good. The Soviets earned their way into the final with a 4–2 win over Sweden, avenging their round-robin loss to the defending runners-up.

Having provided hockey fans with the championship they wanted, the Canadians and Soviets wasted little time

putting on a show in the best-of-three final. Mike Gartner opened the Game 1 scoring for Canada before the Soviets poured it on. Alexi Kasatonov tied the score, Vladimir Krutov put the Russians ahead, Sergei Makarov made it 3–1 on a shorthanded breakaway, and Valeri Kamensky scored from just inside the blue line to make it 4–1. The Forum fans fell silent.

Canada closed the gap in the final minute of the second period on a deflected shot from Bourque. Gilmour made it 4–3 early in the third, and Glenn Anderson evened it shortly after. Gretzky capped the incredible comeback, swiping the puck off Russian netminder Sergei Mylnikov and into the net.

The Soviets staged their own comeback, and this one decided the game. A fluke deflection beat Fuhr to force overtime, and Alexander Semak ended things early in the extra period, whipping a wrist shot past Fuhr's glove.

The loss left fans and players disheartened.

"Canada never lost its wish to be recognized as the world's most dominant hockey power," said Strachan. "In a sense, these were exhibition games, but this event was taken very seriously."

Canada struck quickly in Game 2, with Gilmour, Coffey, and Normand Rochefort giving the home side a 3–1 lead. Fetisov closed the gap, and Krutov evened the score with a short-handed goal. Canada regained the lead and held it until the third period, when Vyacheslav Bykov scored to make it 4–4.

Lemieux restored the one-goal margin before Kamensky forced a second straight OT, splitting the Canadian defence and jousting the puck past Fuhr while falling to the ice. Facing elimination, the Canadians poured on the pressure, evening the series when Lemieux wristed a shot into a partially open net in the second OT.

With tensions at a boiling point, Canada came out flat in Game 3 as the Soviets struck for three goals in the opening eight minutes. Forced into another emotional comeback, the Canadians came through with goals by Brian Propp and Rick Tocchet to move to within one. Andrei Khomutov briefly deflated the comeback, sliding a backhander past Fuhr.

Larry Murphy's goal cut the lead to 4–3, and Brent Sutter's one-timer from the high slot evened the score. Hawerchuk gave Canada its first lead soon after, banging home a loose puck. The Canadians had crawled back from the brink once again—and once again, the Soviets spoiled the party. Semak one-timed a pass into the Canadian net, making it 5–5 with seven and a half minutes left in regulation.

Overtime loomed for the third straight night, with the Canadians preparing for a faceoff in their own zone with under two minutes remaining. Hawerchuk won the draw, then tied up a Russian forward. Lemieux then poked the puck past the Soviet defenceman to start a three-on-one with Gretzky and Murphy. Gretzky gathered up the puck down the left side, while Murphy darted for the goal.

Mylnikov bought the decoy, leaving Gretzky to make a perfect drop pass to the trailing Lemieux, who whistled a wrist shot past a stumbling Mylnikov.

The Soviets could not score the tying goal, and as members of Team Canada celebrated, fans across the country joined them. The 1987 Canada Cup would never equal the drama of the 1972 Summit Series, but it may have been the best display of hockey the world has ever seen.

"The 1987 series was really special," said Gretzky. "It was really neat that we lost, then came back and won two straight. It was a great series, and I'm glad I was a part of it."

The Canadian Press/Chuck Stoody

GREENE MEANS GO(LD) (1968)

AS A YOUNG NANCY GREENE watched teammate Anne Heggtveit win gold at the 1960 Olympics in Squaw Valley, Calif., the Canadian skier vowed to do the same one day.

Eight years later, Greene made good on her promise, capping an outstanding career with a record-smashing victory at the 1968 Games in Grenoble, France. Canada's queen of the slopes dominated the sport in her prime, solidifying her place as the greatest women's skier in North American history.

Greene hit the slopes the moment she was old enough to do so. She and her five siblings all took up the sport at age three, and their parents were founding members of a B.C. ski club. Greene took up ski racing in high school, and showed immediate promise—as a 15-year-old, she placed second to her sister Elizabeth at the Canadian

junior championship in her native Rossland despite being one of the more inexperienced competitors in the event. A sibling rivalry quickly developed, one which made both skiers better.

A year later, Greene joined the national ski team and qualified for the 1960 Olympics. Realizing she was still a relative newcomer to competitive skiing, Greene was meticulous in her training regimen, skiing the same hills over and over again in order to hone her skills and develop the stamina she would need to compete with the world's best. Greene prided herself on being the centre of attention as a young girl in Rossland—and she had every intention of doing the same thing on the world stage.

Greene's initial Olympic results showed tremendous promise, though Greene was far from satisfied with them. She was just 16 when she competed in Squaw Valley, placing twenty-second in the downhill, twenty-sixth in the giant slalom, and thirty-first in the slalom.

Yet, while Greene brushed her own performance aside, she was delighted to have the opportunity to see Heggtveit's gold-medal run up close. Greene roomed with the Olympic champion in Squaw Valley, and saw firsthand what it took to win the biggest event in the world. From that moment, Greene made it her mandate to top the podium at an Olympic Games, and serve as her own inspiration to younger skiers.

Four years later, Greene headed to the Olympics in Innsbruck, Austria, with high hopes for herself. Yet, while her seventh-place result in the downhill was the best by any North American in the competition, it wasn't the podium finish she desired. Coupled with a fifteenth-place result in the slalom and a sixteenth-place showing in the giant slalom, Greene returned home dejected.

"I was disappointed for sure," said Greene. "At the time, I thought I had a chance to win a medal, and that's what I was aiming for. In hindsight, I know I wasn't ready."

The Associated Press

Greene used her position as one of the country's top skiers to lobby for drastic improvements to the country's fledgling ski program. Greene believed the Canadian team needed more events in Europe, where the top skiers in the world plied their craft. Her wish was granted, and Canada instantly became more competitive in international events. The creation of a World Cup, a series of events featuring the world's elite downhill racers, gave Greene extra motivation to be the best—and it didn't take long for her to reach the pinnacle of her sport.

Greene's continued improvement led to the podium results she had yearned for throughout her career. Greene quickly found herself climbing the women's world rankings, earning the inaugural World Cup title, and with it the 1967 Lou Marsh Trophy as Canada's athlete of the year. Her victory marked the third straight time a woman had won the award, galvanizing Canada's place as one of the strongest training grounds for women's athletics in the entire world.

One month before the Grenoble Games, Greene's Olympic dreams nearly came to a crashing halt. She slipped during a training run in Bad Gastein, Austria, and wiped out, badly pulling the ligaments in her right ankle. Canadian fans groaned at the news, remaining optimistic but fearing the worst.

Yet, despite the severity of the injury, Greene's confidence never wavered.

"I knew that I had enough time to recover," said Greene. "It was just a question of doing the physiotherapy. I was already confident in my technical abilities, and I felt like if I didn't make any mistakes, I should win."

Greene was a distant tenth in the downhill race, more than two seconds slower than gold-medal winner Olga Pall of Austria. After three days of introspection, Greene arrived at the slopes with a cautious optimism about her chance at a medal in the slalom. She whisked down the course in one minute, 26.15 seconds, less than three-tenths off Marielle Goitschel's winning time.

The silver-medal result thrilled fans back home, but left Greene unsatisfied. Winning Canada's third-ever alpine medal was nice, but it wasn't gold. And it left her still unfulfilled in her quest to top the podium, a vow she'd made to herself eight years earlier.

Her ninth and final chance at Olympic glory came in the giant slalom competition on February 15. Greene was relaxed, but intent on attacking the Chamrousse course with everything she had. The ninth skier out of the gate, Greene rocketed down the course, making each turn with unparalleled precision. Her form remained perfect well past the halfway point, and she maintained her blistering pace for every step of the 1,610-metre course.

As she crossed the finish line, her official time remained a mystery due to a scoreboard malfunction. Several anxiety-filled moments later, the board lit up: one minute, 51.97 seconds. Greene wound up beating silver medallist Annie Famose of France by 2.64 seconds in one of the most dominant performances in the history of the sport.

"For those few seconds, I actually thought, 'Oh dear, they've missed my time,'" said Greene. "Once the time finally came up, I felt a great deal of relief and joy. I knew I had skied a great run."

Greene won seven World Cup races that season, capturing her second straight World Cup title. That earned her a second consecutive Lou Marsh Award, making her the first athlete to win two straight since Barbara Ann Scott 20 years earlier. Greene would retire immediately following the 1968 season, going out on top of the world at just 24 years old.

More than three decades later, Greene was selected Canada's Female Athlete of the Century in a vote of broadcasters and newspaper editors from across the country. Despite spending less than a decade of her life in competition, Rossland's golden child was recognized as the greatest sportswoman her country had ever produced.

GRETZKY BECOMES NHL'S SCORING KING (1989)

EVERYBODY KNEW WAYNE GRETZKY would become hockey's all-time scoring leader—it was only a matter of when.

Whether by coincidence or fate, the Los Angeles Kings centre was in position to reach the mark in Edmonton, the city where he first became a superstar after leading the Oilers to four Stanley Cup titles. Gretzky's career had been littered with magical moments, and October 15, 1989, was no different as "The Great One" scored in the final minute of regulation for his 1,851st career point, making him the most prolific scorer in NHL history.

"Everything I accomplished was because of the Oilers and the city of Edmonton," says Gretzky. "It was just by chance that I was able to break the record right there in Edmonton."

The city's love affair with the skinny kid from Brantford, Ont., began immediately after he arrived in the Alberta capital. His lone season in the World Hockey Association saw him record 104 points in the regular season and another 20 in the playoffs. When the Oilers joined the National Hockey League the following season, Gretzky went with them, giving the franchise an immediate superstar.

After opening his NHL career with a 137-point campaign, Gretzky spent the next seven years annihilating the league's record books. He established new single-season marks in goals (92), assists (163), and points (215). During a five-year stretch from 1981–1986, Gretzky reached the 200-point plateau four times—a mark no other player has ever reached—and came up four points shy in the other season. He also set new records for assists (31) and points (47) in a single post-season while leading the team to its first three Stanley Cup championships.

Many other records fell during Gretzky's tenure in Edmonton. He reached the 50-goal plateau in 39 games, 11 faster than any other player in history—and he did

it as a 20-year-old. His 51-game points streak remains the longest in the history of the league, and he was the fastest to the 100-point mark (34 games). His play put Edmonton on the map, making the Oilers one of the most recognized franchises in all of North America.

The 1987–88 season ended with Gretzky celebrating a fourth Stanley Cup title in Edmonton, though he finished second in league scoring to Mario Lemieux while failing to score 50 goals for the first time in his career. Nonetheless, Gretzky had increased his career point total to 1,669 (583 goals, 1,086 assists) in just 696 games, and was poised to pass the legendary Gordie Howe before his thirtieth birthday.

Howe recalls meeting Gretzky while he was a young boy, and knew right away he would be something special.

"You had to fall in love with the kid and his thoughts on hockey," says Howe. "He wouldn't take his eye off you when you talked to him about hockey. You know when a kid looks at you with those wide eyes, you know he's going to improve."

Gretzky and Howe each enjoyed superstardom in their respective eras, though Gretzky benefited greatly from playing in an era with an increased emphasis on offence. Howe had established the league scoring mark

through 26 seasons of grinding and plugging. He had just one 100-point season, and it came in his twenty-third NHL campaign. Howe needed more than 1,750 games to amass 1,850 career points—Gretzky was on pace to do it in less than half the time.

By the late 1980s, Gretzky had already won three Lou Marsh awards as Canadian athlete of the year. The country had never seen an athlete like him, a brilliant scorer and playmaker with a million-dollar smile, the ideal ambassador for his sport and for the country as a whole.

And just like that, he was bound for Tinseltown.

On request from "The Great One" himself, Oilers owner Peter Pocklington shipped Gretzky, Marty McSorley, and Mike Krushelnyski to the Los Angeles Kings for Jimmy Carson, Martin Gelinas, three first-round draft picks, and $15 million. The deal allowed Gretzky to start a new life in California with his new wife, actress Janet Jones. The trade also provided the Oilers with a much-needed influx of cash they could use to retain other key players like Mark Messier, Grant Fuhr, and Paul Coffey.

Gretzky's 168-point performance in his first season in L.A. left him just 13 shy of Howe by the start of the 1989–90 season. The Kings would play their sixth game of the regular season in Edmonton, leaving an outside chance that Gretzky might set the mark against his former team. Seemingly inspired by the opportunity, Gretzky began the season on a tear, recording 12 points over his first five games. A three-assist effort in a 6–5 win over Vancouver left Gretzky needing just one point in Edmonton to tie the record.

Gretzky didn't disappoint the sellout crowd at Northlands Coliseum, assisting on Bernie Nicholls's goal 4:32 into the first period for the record-tying point. Gretzky had several chances to break the record, but couldn't beat Edmonton netminder Bill Ranford. A second-period knock to the head nearly kept him out for the entire third period. And with the Oilers clinging to a 4–3 lead late in the game, it appeared Gretzky's 1,851st point would come elsewhere.

With the Kings' netminder on the bench for an extra man, Kings forward Dave Taylor deflected defenceman Steve Duchesne's cross-ice pass right to Gretzky, who whistled a backhand past Ranford for the history-making goal. Gretzky leapt in celebration as the fans gave him a five-minute standing ovation. He hadn't worn the orange, blue, and white in 17 months, but to fans in the Alberta capital, Gretzky would always be an Edmonton Oiler.

By the time Gretzky suited up for his final NHL game in 1999 as a member of the New York Rangers, the legendary centre had left Howe and the rest of the league in his dust. Gretzky finished with 894 career goals and 1,963 assists, and would have been the all-time scoring leader even if the league had only counted his helpers. He ended his career with a lead of more than 1,000 points over his next closest competitor, the proud owner of 61 NHL records, four Stanley Cup championships, and a hockey legacy that will never be matched.

Gretzky cherishes the all-time scoring record, but says Howe's accomplishments shouldn't be overlooked. "I'm proud to hold the record, and to have accomplished what I did," he said. "But there should be an asterisk beside it. I played under a completely different system than Gordie Howe did. There should be two scoring marks—mine, and Gordie's."

TERRY FOX'S MARATHON OF HOPE (1980)

TERRY FOX BECAME a national icon simply by doing what he did best—running.

Fox began his Marathon of Hope as a 21-year-old amputee with a dream of crossing the nation on foot to raise awareness and money for cancer research. And though Fox wasn't able to finish the coast-to-coast trek, his story provided inspiration for all Canadians, touching millions of lives while generating millions of dollars for his cause.

"I think it would be a mistake for those that are sort of embedding Terry's story in history to put him so far on a pedestal that they remove his true story," says close friend Rick Hansen. "For Canadians who are looking for hope and inspiration, Terry was someone at eye level, not someone who was a superstar."

Born in Winnipeg and raised in Vancouver, Fox was an athlete at heart. His foray into organized sports began in earnest in junior high, when Fox enjoyed a number of pastimes, including basketball. Though he wasn't a good player early on, Fox worked on his skills daily, eventually becoming the starting point guard for Port Coquitlam High School. He shared athlete-of-the-year honours in his final year of high school, and graduated with distinction.

Fox loved physical activity so much, he enrolled in kinesiology at Simon Fraser University with the hope of becoming a physical education teacher. Fox impressed coaches at the school with his enthusiasm, and he participated in a number of campus clubs and organizations. Life was indeed good for the young man with the infectious smile.

Fox's life took a tragic turn in March 1977, after coming home with a sore knee following a track session. Fox was taken to a New Westminster, B.C., hospital, where he was diagnosed as having osteogenic sarcoma, a type of bone cancer often found in children or young adults.

To prevent the spread of the disease, doctors amputated Fox's right leg 15 centimetres above the knee.

Fox wouldn't let the cancer affect his ability to compete. He was playing golf less than two months after the amputation, and later played basketball with the Canadian Wheelchair Sports Association, where he first met Hansen. Fox went on to enjoy three national titles with the team, showing an aptitude that surprised teammates and coaches alike. After being fitted with a better prosthetic leg, Fox participated in a marathon in Prince George, B.C., finishing last in the field. But Fox, and those who clapped, cheered, and cried for him at the finish line, didn't care where he placed. He finished the race, and that was all that mattered.

Though he was encouraged by his drive and determination to overcome the cancer that had ravaged his leg, he was appalled by what he considered to be inadequate cancer treatment in Canada. So, in 1979, he devised a plan to raise $24 million for cancer research, one dollar for every man, woman, and child in the country.

He would run from coast to coast.

Reaction to his quest was lukewarm initially, but support grew gradually as friends and family realized that Fox was going through with it, no matter what. The Canadian Cancer Society was eager to lend a hand, but only if Fox was able to track down corporate sponsors. Seeing it as simply the latest in a series of challenges he had faced in his life, Fox enlisted the help of a number of companies, including Imperial Oil, Adidas, and Ford. His family helped raise money for expenses Fox would face during his journey, and before long he was counting down the days to his cross-country jaunt. Having run more than 5,000 kilometres in training, Fox knew he was ready to face his most enormous task to date.

On April 12, 1980, Fox dabbed his artificial leg into the cold Atlantic Ocean in St. John's, Nfld., and began the Marathon of Hope. A small crowd, a police escort, and close friend Doug Alward greeted him as he departed the Newfoundland capital bound for the Pacific.

Newfoundlanders opened their arms and their wallets for Fox, donating whatever they could afford. He made it through Prince Edward Island rapidly and then headed off to traverse the rest of Atlantic Canada. Things became tense at times between Fox and Alward, with the two men bickering constantly. Despite the growing animosity, they trudged on, and when things finally cooled off Fox expressed his gratitude to Alward for sticking it out even when times were tough.

Later in the year, Fox was named a Companion to the Order of Canada, and captured the Lou Marsh Award as the nation's athlete of the year. The tour had long been finished, but the donations continued pouring in as Canadians paid tribute to Fox's amazing spirit. By February 1981, he had reached his goal of $1 raised per Canadian.

Fox died on June 28, 1981, a month before his twenty-third birthday, and the first official Terry Fox Run was held that September. Over the next quarter-century, the foundation in his name would raise over $400 million for cancer research. And every fall, hundreds of thousands of Canadians lace up the sneakers, hit the streets, and follow in Fox's legendary footsteps, celebrating one of the most heroic achievements in the nation's history.

"Just think what might not have happened if he didn't dip his leg in the Atlantic Ocean and head westward," said Hansen. "We can only imagine what society has lost. And even when he finally had to stop, the rest of the country kept his dream alive.

"It just shows us that sometimes it's not the destination, it's the journey, giving it your best and not losing sight of what's most important. That's exactly what Terry did."

After struggling with both the language barrier and a pair of motorists who nearly ran him off the road, Fox marched through Quebec and crossed the border into Hawkesbury, Ont., greeted by a thunderous ovation. Shortly after, it was on to Ottawa and a chance to meet Prime Minister Pierre Trudeau. Fox was a superstar by the time he reached Toronto, where approximately 10,000 supporters welcomed him to Nathan Phillips Square.

After celebrating his twenty-second birthday in Gravenhurst, Ont., Fox began to tire. By mid-August his trip was half done, and he had raised over $11 million, putting him on pace to equal or surpass his goal. But he struggled to maintain his daily pace, and on August 31, as he departed Thunder Bay, Ont., he knew something was wrong. Pains in his chest and neck burned with each step, and despite the cheers of encouragement from those along the route, Fox knew his journey was nearly over.

A hospital visit confirmed the worst: the cancer had returned, and was lodged in his lungs. After 5,376 kilometres, Terry Fox's Marathon of Hope came to an end.

NASH REPEATS AS NBA MVP (2006)

THE NOTION OF STEVE NASH as the most valuable player of the National Basketball Association seemed a little strange at first, even to Nash.

Imagine how people felt when he won the award for a second time.

The floppy-haired Canadian point guard stunned the basketball world in the summer of 2006 by capturing league MVP honours for the second consecutive year. In doing so, he became just the third guard to win back-to-back MVP awards, joining Magic Johnson and Michael Jordan. In just two seasons, the personable Nash went from being a veteran guard on the decline to being anointed as one of the best players at his position in the history of the league.

"I think in some ways it has sunk in, and in other ways it will never sink in," said Nash. "I had big dreams growing up, but I never dreamed of being MVP. Some days it's unbelievable that I won."

Nobody—not even Nash himself—could have expected the South African–born, Victoria-raised introvert to become one of the best guards in NBA history, especially because Nash's first love was soccer. He didn't even take up basketball until he was 12, balancing both sports throughout high school. His brother Martin was also a fantastic athlete, and later joined the national men's soccer team.

As for Steve, he preferred basketball throughout high school. His hard work paid off in 1992, when he led St. Michael's University School to the B.C. triple-A championship, taking home provincial player-of-the-year honours in the process. He also led his school's rugby team to a provincial title.

Nash desperately wanted to play Division I basketball in the U.S., but schools simply weren't paying attention to Canadian high school hoops. It took dozens of mailouts to American schools before California's Santa

Clara University came calling, offering Nash a scholarship. It didn't take long for the 1.91-metre-tall point guard to make an impact, leading the Broncos to their first NCAA tournament appearance in five years. If that wasn't impressive enough, Nash hit six free throws in the final minute as Santa Clara, ranked 15th, knocked off the No. 2 Arizona Wildcats in the first round.

Nash spent three more seasons at Santa Clara, and began playing with the Canadian national team during the summer prior to his senior year. Nash finished his Broncos career as a two-time West Coast Conference player of the year, while owning the school record for assists (510) and free-throw percentage (.862). Word had spread: The kid could play. And despite being a Canadian player toiling in a second-tier conference, Nash was selected 15th overall by the Phoenix Suns in the 1996 NBA draft.

The first two seasons of Nash's NBA career were spent largely on the bench. Nash played in 65 games in his rookie campaign but averaged just 10.5 minutes per game behind incumbent Jason Kidd and veteran Kevin Johnson. His time in Arizona came to an abrupt end shortly after the 1998 draft, when he was shipped to the Dallas Mavericks in a four-player trade. Nash would go from part-time player to newly minted starter—and superstardom would follow.

Nash's first two seasons with the Mavericks provided glimpses into his immense potential. Though Nash wasn't yet a top-flight player, he did average more than five as-

sists per game over that span as the Mavericks began their slow climb out of the Western Conference doldrums. In his third year in Dallas, Nash finally reached the upper echelon of NBA point guards, averaging 15.6 points and 7.3 rebounds as the Mavericks reached the playoffs for the first time in 11 years.

Nash continued his emergence as an elite point guard with the Mavericks, earning a pair of all-star nods and helping guide the team to the top of the Western Conference standings, yet he couldn't lead the Mavericks over the hump, failing to reach the NBA final in his six years in Dallas. A first-round loss to the Sacramento Kings in the 2003–04 playoffs was especially disheartening.

Nash became a free agent in the summer of 2004, and many believed he would remain in Dallas. But Mavericks owner Mark Cuban was hesitant to give Nash a long contract, apprehensive about the point guard's back problems. While Cuban offered four years, the Phoenix Suns dangled a six-year deal in front of him.

In a flash, Nash returned to the team that had drafted him.

Phoenix's nucleus was one of the league's youngest, and the team had posted an uninspiring 29–53 record the year before. With Nash at the helm, the Suns orchestrated the most dramatic turnaround in NBA history. Phoenix walloped the league, posting a 62–20 record while averaging over 110 points per game.

"I definitely felt like it was a great fit," said Nash. "With the pieces they already had there, I thought we could post a winning record. I expected success, but I certainly didn't think we would double our win total."

Nash had a season for the record books, averaging 15.5 points and a league-high 11.5 assists, the league's highest average in a decade. His role as the Suns' ringleader earned Nash a narrow victory over Shaquille O'Neal in the MVP voting. Nash became the first Canadian to earn the honour, and copped the Lou Marsh Award as Canada's top athlete.

The following season saw major changes in Phoenix. All-star big man Amare Stoudemire would miss the majority of the season with a knee injury. Talented guard Joe Johnson was sent to Atlanta for Boris Diaw. Three-point specialist Quentin Richardson was jettisoned to New York for forward Kurt Thomas.

With such significant roster turnover, few expected the Suns to repeat their magic from the previous season. Nash relished the challenge.

"Instead of crying about it, we kept moving forward," said Nash. "We focused on doing the best we could with the players we had. And we were a tight unit."

Nash enjoyed one of the best shooting seasons in NBA history, becoming just the fourth player to average 50 percent from the field, 40 percent from three-point range, and 90 percent from the free-throw line. His scoring average (18.8) was a career high, and he still dished out 10.5 assists. Nash was an all-star starter for the first time, leading the Suns to 54 wins and a second straight berth in the conference final.

Nash held off Cleveland Cavaliers superstar LeBron James to become just the ninth back-to-back MVP winner in history. When Nash accepted the Maurice Podoloff Trophy for a second time, he entered an elite class of multi-time MVPs, which included Michael Jordan, Wilt Chamberlain, Larry Bird, and Kareem Abdul-Jabbar.

"You talk to scouts today, and they're all looking for the next Steve Nash," said Toronto Raptors play-by-play man Chuck Swirsky. "It really endorses all of the amazing things he's accomplished."

The Canadian Press/COC/Andre

CANADIAN MEN END OLYMPIC HOCKEY DROUGHT (2002)

A $1 DEPOSIT PROVED TO BE the best investment in Canadian Olympic history.

The ice maker at the 2002 Olympic hockey tournament, an Edmonton native, buried a loonie in the Salt Lake City ice prior to the start of the event. With the Canadian men's team in the throes of a 50-year gold-medal drought, a little superstition couldn't hurt.

While the coin had nothing to do with the ultimate outcome, it provided an entertaining sidebar for one of the most emotional victories of the Games. With a 5–3 victory over the U.S. in the championship game, Canada put an end to a series of disappointments, near-misses, and embarrassments that spanned five decades.

The Associated Press/Kevork Djansezian

The Canadian Press/COC/Andre Forget

"After 50 years of not winning a gold medal, to go in and rally to win the championship, it was definitely a special moment," said Wayne Gretzky, the team's executive director. "I would put the 2002 Olympics and the 1987 Canada Cup win in the same category."

From the outset of the tournament, the pressure on the Canadian team was immense. Four years earlier in Nagano, Japan, Canada rolled through the round-robin

and quarter-final before dropping a 2-1 shootout decision to the Czech Republic, who went on to win gold. The Canadians settled for a fourth-place finish, a dismal result for the pre-tournament favourites—especially considering this was the first Olympics to feature professional players, a decision thought to give Canada a decided advantage.

While those involved in the Nagano mess tried to figure out what went wrong, Hockey Canada adopted a more aggressive approach to the 2002 Olympic tournament in Salt Lake City. Wayne Gretzky, who was in uniform for the Canadian team in Japan, was named executive director for the 2002 edition. He quickly lined up an all-star coaching staff, with Pat Quinn leading the way and Ken Hitchcock and Wayne Fleming serving as his assistants. Gretzky and the three coaches were called upon to lead Canada to its first Olympic men's hockey gold in exactly 50 years.

They certainly had the right players for the job.

Legendary centre Mario Lemieux was named team captain, 15 years after he and Gretzky joined forces to lead Canada to the 1987 Canada Cup championship. He

The Canadian Press/Paul Chiasson

was joined up front by veterans Joe Sakic, Steve Yzerman, Theo Fleury, Joe Nieuwendyk, and Brendan Shanahan. Jarome Iginla and Simon Gagne provided a necessary influx of youth on the wings. Al MacInnis and Rob Blake anchored a towering blue-line which included former Hart Trophy winner Chris Pronger and his future Stanley Cup teammate Scott Niedermayer. Martin Brodeur, Ed Belfour, and Curtis Joseph made up the goaltending trifecta.

The Canadian Press/Frank Gunn

Despite icing an intimidating lineup, the Canadians were far from guaranteed a spot on the podium. Canada was just one of six teams expected to contend for a medal, joined by the host Americans, Russia, Sweden, Finland, and the Czech Republic. Each team had a wealth of NHL talent, meaning there would be no easy path to the gold-medal game. And with each team having to play a quarter-final game prior to the medal round, a bad game at the wrong time would mean another four years of futility for the hungry Canadians.

Following the trend of national teams getting off to awful starts, Canada dropped its opening game 5–2 to Sweden. Though the players knew the round-robin was just a pre-playoff warm-up, the loss to the Swedes was alarming. Quinn was astonished at how out of sync the Canadians looked, having watched a 1-1 tie evaporate on the strength of four second-period goals by the Swedes. Though every team left in the tournament would reach the playoffs, it seemed all too likely that the Canadians were in for a difficult quarter-final matchup.

A 3–2 victory over Germany and a 3–3 draw with the Czech Republic drove the mild-mannered Gretzky into an uncharacteristic tirade. Gretzky lashed out following

the Czech game, accusing other nations of hating Canada and rooting for his team to fail. While the claims seemed a little over the top, the outburst gave the players a sorely needed boost.

"Wayne is sincere—he obviously felt that way," said longtime Olympic broadcaster Brian Williams. "There was no phoniness to that. The players looked to him and rallied around him, and I think the speech had a great effect."

Thanks to an unspectacular 1–1–1 round-robin record, Canada's gold-medal route was not going to be an easy one. First came the Finns, who knocked off the Russians 3–1 in round-robin play and looked strong in doing so. The Canadians knew they would need to tighten up on defence, and they did, squeaking out a 2–1 victory on goals by Sakic and Yzerman.

Canada snagged its biggest break of the tournament when Belarus pulled off a stunner in the round of eight, upsetting Sweden 4–3. The result meant that Canada had a date with the underdog Belarussians in one semifinal, while Russia and the U.S. tangled in the other.

Canada left little to chance, breaking open a 1–1 game with six unanswered goals in a 7–1 romp that easily

The Canadian Press/COC/Andre Forget

qualified as the team's best performance of the tournament. The United States' 3–2 win over Russia made it an all–North American Olympic final for the first time since the 1960 Games in Squaw Valley, Calif. The American victory came exactly 22 years after the "Miracle on Ice," a game which saw the U.S. stun the heavily favoured Soviets en route to Olympic gold. The hosts were hoping lightning would strike again.

Tony Amonte put the Americans on the board 8:49 into the first period, bringing the sellout crowd to its feet. Two of Canada's young guns replied, with Paul Kariya tying the score at 14:54 and Iginla converting a Sakic pass less than four minutes later. Canada nursed the 2–1 lead through 20 minutes.

After both teams exchanged multiple scoring chances, including one where Lemieux missed a wide-open net, U.S. defenceman Brian Rafalski tied the score on a power play at 15:30 of the second, with MacInnis in the penalty box for interference. Sakic restored the lead less than three minutes later, wristing a shot past U.S. goalie Mike Richter from the top of the left circle. With two periods in the books, Canada had a 3–2 lead.

The Americans pressed relentlessly for the tying goal, but Brodeur was impenetrable, his best save coming on a Brett Hull slapshot that nearly whistled inside the near post. Less than a minute later, Iginla wired an Yzerman feed past Richter to give Canada a critical two-goal advantage with just under four minutes left. Sakic added his second of the game on a breakaway at 18:40, and the celebration was on.

An elated Gretzky dug the $1 coin out of the ice after the game and had it sent to the Hockey Hall of Fame, but not before celebrating a truly golden moment on the golden anniversary of Canada's last Olympic hockey triumph.

MIKE WEIR WINS MASTERS (2003)

MIKE WEIR MAY BE the only golfer to earn a standing ovation at a hockey game.

Fans greeted Weir with nearly a minute of applause as he took part in a ceremonial faceoff between the Toronto Maple Leafs and the Philadelphia Flyers. One day before dropping the puck, Weir dropped a putt that would earn him a special place in Canadian golf history. A tap-in bogey on the first playoff hole earned him a victory over Len Mattiace at the 2003 Masters, making the Bright's Grove, Ont., native the first Canadian PGA golfer to ever win a professional major.

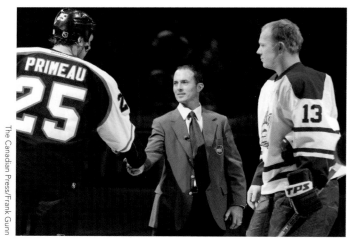

Weir paid his dues in the early- and mid-1990s, toiling away on the Canadian Tour after a successful career at Utah's Brigham Young University that saw him win Western Athletic Conference Player of the Year in 1992. He won the Infinity Tournament Players Championship in 1993, helping him earn Canadian Tour rookie-of-the-year honours. Things were looking up for Weir, but he just couldn't break into the PGA Tour.

His first big break came in 1997, when he won the Canadian Tour's Order of Merit with victories at the BC TEL Pacific Open and the Canadian Masters—an event Weir captured with a tournament-record score of 18 under. He also led the tour in scoring average, earning his way onto the PGA Tour. He promptly lost his card after finishing 131st on the money list in 1998, just six places short of the cutoff.

Having worked so hard to reach the PGA Tour in the first place, the competitive lefty wasn't about to slip back into obscurity. Weir not only made the cutoff at the season-ending PGA qualifying school, he won the entire tournament, taking home $50,000 for his efforts. Weir was headed back to the PGA Tour—and this time, he was sticking around.

Weir posted four top-5 finishes in 1999, capped by an emotional victory at the Air Canada Championship in September. The triumph earned Weir $450,000, helping him to a 23rd-place finish on the PGA Tour's money list. There would be no returning to the Canadian Tour for Weir, who was quickly gaining support as Canada's next big name in golf.

His 2000 season featured eight top-10 results, including Weir's biggest payday to date—a $1-million victory at the American Express Championship, the final event of the season. That vaulted him into sixth place on the money list, and 21st in the world rankings. Weir was also invited to compete in his first-ever Presidents Cup competition, where he boasted a record of 3–2–0 for the International Team. His sensational season earned him the Canadian Press Male Athlete of the Year award.

Weir would go on to earn more than $3.5 million over his next two seasons, though he took a step back in 2002 by going without a victory. Fans wondered if Weir would ever be able to capture a major championship, something no Canadian men's golfer had ever done before. Weir certainly gave them reason to believe early in his 2003 season, earning victories three weeks apart at the Bob Hope Chrysler Classic and the Nissan Open.

Playing the best golf of his career, Weir headed to the Masters with victory on his mind.

The Augusta National course was soaked from a steady rain, which wiped out play on the opening day. That meant having to play up to 36 holes on Friday, something Weir wasn't looking forward to, especially at a major.

"The course played long for everybody," said Weir. "I think being in good shape played a bit of a factor, especially on such a hilly golf course. Sometimes a physical slip can lead to a mental slip."

Weir fired a 70 in his opening round and followed it up with a stunning 68 in round two, which began Friday afternoon and ended Saturday morning. Midway through the Masters, Weir had a whopping four-shot lead.

Everything changed in a 90-minute span of the third round, when Weir watched a five-shot advantage vanish into the Georgia air. Jeff Maggert passed the lefty with birdies on Nos. 17 and 18, though Weir drew even with his own birdie on No. 15. He followed by bogeying Nos. 16 and 17, completing a dreadful 75, which dropped him two shots back heading into Sunday's final round.

Weir hoped his worst performance was already behind him.

"My mindset didn't change, and neither did my game plan," says Weir. "I can't rear back and gain an extra 30 yards like some guys can when they need to. My game is about precision. And I wasn't going to let one bad round change my approach."

Weir began Sunday with a birdie on No. 2, and found himself back in the lead after Maggert took a disastrous triple-bogey on the third hole. The advantage was short-lived, through little fault of Weir's—Len Mattiace had come out of nowhere with a birdie barrage that gave him a three-shot lead at one point.

Weir birdied No. 13 to close the gap to two shots. Another birdie on the par-5 15th coincided with a Mattiace bogey on 18, and Weir was back into a tie for the lead. He went on to force a playoff by saving par on each of the final three holes, capped by a knee-knocking putt on No. 18.

"He took no time over that putt," said longtime golf reporter Bob Weeks. "It was like he just knew he was going to make it. He had a tremendous amount of confidence going into the playoff."

Weir and Mattiace headed to No. 10 for the first playoff hole. After both men hit clean drives, Mattiace sprayed his approach shot to the left, winding up behind a tree. Weir's second shot found the front side of the green, roughly 15 metres from the hole.

Mattiace's third shot left him with a difficult chip, and he buzzed the ball nearly 9 metres past the hole. Weir hit his putt to within 1 metre, while Mattiace two-putted for a double-bogey. Weir missed his par opportunity but still had a tap-in for the championship.

As Weir knocked the ball into the cup, he raised both arms in the air, shook Mattiace's hand, and gave caddie Brennan Little an enormous hug. A near-perfect final round gave Weir the biggest win of his professional career.

"There was a sense of relief that went through every fibre of my being when I realized that, through days of distractions and weather delays, I was able to be focused and not lose sight of my goal," says Weir. "I was most proud that I was able to do that and come out on top."

Weir's victory earned him a permanent fan following in Canada, where even members of the Toronto Maple Leafs shook his hand in awe.

It would have been a bigger thrill for Weir—but he's a Detroit Red Wings fan.

The Associated Press/Hans Deryk

BLUE JAYS ON TOP OF THE WORLD—AGAIN (1993)

SKYDOME NEVER KNEW what hit it.

As Joe Carter golfed a Mitch Williams pitch deep down the left-field line, the crowd of over 54,000 fans bolted to its feet. The ball cleared the wall and the stadium erupted as Carter danced around the bases, leaping into a mob of teammates at home plate. The Blue Jays had become the first team in 16 years to repeat as World Series champions, and the ensuing hoopla shook every inch of the 'Dome.

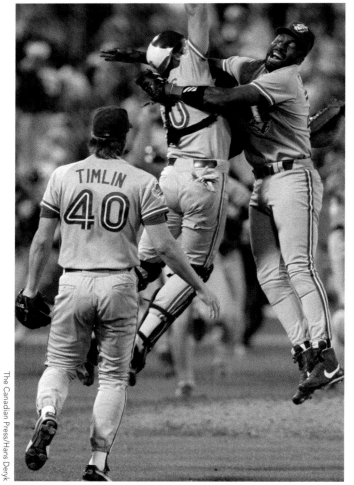

The Canadian Press/Hans Deryk

"The way it ended, you couldn't have scripted it any better," said Hall of Famer Paul Molitor, who took home World Series MVP honours while earning his first championship ring. "To finally be a world champion after 16 years understatedly was an awesome feeling."

Toronto's first world championship was impressive enough on its own. The Blue Jays opened the 1992 season with six consecutive victories, and didn't lose two in a row until the end of April. Toronto never really found itself in any trouble right up until the all-star break, hitting the mid-season mark at 50–31.

A dreadful August (14–16) gave way to a scintillating September and October (21–9) as the Jays captured their third American East title in the previous four years. Toronto showed remarkable consistency, having completed the season without ever being swept in a series. Jack Morris posted 21 victories in his second full season with the Jays, while free-agent addition and future Hall of Famer Dave Winfield provided serious pop in the designated-hitter spot.

The Jays met the Oakland Athletics in the American League Championship Series. After taking a 2–1 series lead, Toronto found itself down 6–1 in Game 4 in Oakland. The Jays scored three times in the eighth inning before Roberto Alomar swatted a two-run homer off A's closer Dennis Eckersley. Toronto would go on to win 7–6 in 11 innings, taking a 3–1 lead in a series. The Jays got past Oakland in six games to advance to their first World Series against the Atlanta Braves.

After splitting the first two games in Georgia, Toronto returned home to a raucous SkyDome and won two of three, carrying a 3–2 series lead back to Atlanta. The Jays appeared to have the game won before surrendering the tying run in the bottom of the ninth. Winfield then delivered the crushing blow two innings later, smacking a two-run double down the left-field line. The Braves

reduced the lead to 4–3, but Mike Timlin retired Otis Nixon on a bunt down the first-base line to give Toronto its first-ever world championship.

Though the core of the team remained intact, two key members of the 1992 team headed elsewhere. Winfield signed on with the Minnesota Twins, while closer Tom Henke headed back to the Texas Rangers, with whom he began his career in 1982. The Jays signed Molitor to take Winfield's place in the lineup, and added free-agent starter Dave Stewart, who had a reputation as one of the best playoff pitchers in the league.

The Jays opened their title defence with a flop, sitting at 16–17 as late as early May, before going on a 17–6 stretch that included six- and seven-game winning streaks.

The mid-season months saw the Jays hold off numerous challenges from the Yankees. After dropping to 78–63 on September 9, the Jays ripped off 16 wins in their next 18 games to cruise to their third straight division title.

John Olerud won the batting title, while Molitor and Alomar finished second and third, respectively, in the batting race. Carter added 33 home runs and 121 RBIs, while Pat Hentgen led a solid pitching staff with a 19–9 mark.

Toronto appeared primed for another solid postseason run, and the fans were ready. Over 4 million of them crammed into the 'Dome that season, breaking the record set the previous year.

Molitor expected big crowds, but even he was impressed by the turnout.

"[I was] not really surprised, the fans of the Jays kind of evolved as the franchise did," said Molitor. "But 4 million people was more than anyone could have imagined."

The Jays were in tough in their American League Championship Series with the Chicago White Sox, but prevailed in six games. Stewart earned a pair of wins to take home series MVP honours, and the Jays were on their way back to the World Series.

The Canadian Press/Frank Gunn

The Phillies were the adversaries, having gone 97–65 in the regular season before knocking off the Braves in the NLCS. The SkyDome crowd could barely sit still during Game 1, as the home team broke open a close game with three runs in the seventh inning of an 8–5 win. The Phillies answered back with a 6–4 victory in Game 2, seizing home-field advantage.

Toronto quickly returned the favour, blasting the Phillies for 13 hits in a 10–3 rout. What followed was one of the wildest games in the history of the World Series. Down 14–9 in the eighth inning, the Jays scored six times, capped by a two-run triple from Devon White, to escape with a 15–14 victory, and a 3–1 series lead. Philadelphia held its ground with a 2–0 triumph in Game 5,

meaning the Jays would have two chances to wrap up their second world championship in Toronto.

The Jays scored three times in the first inning, and were cruising with a 5–1 lead through six. But Stewart struggled in the seventh, allowing a three-run homer to Dykstra before leaving the game. Reliever Danny Cox couldn't stop the bleeding, allowing the Phillies to tack on two more runs. All of a sudden, Philadelphia had a 6–5 lead.

It lasted until the ninth inning, when Williams was called upon to close things out. Legendary speedster Rickey Henderson, a mid-season acquisition by the Jays, immediately drew a four-pitch walk, and after White flied out to centre, Alomar drove a single up the middle to put two runners on.

The rest is Canadian sports history.

With the count at two balls and two strikes, Williams delivered a low fastball that Carter hammered into the left-field bullpen, just the second time in baseball history the World Series had ended with a homer. With the 'Dome rocking well after the final pitch was thrown, the Jays were crowned World Series champions for a second straight time, giving Canada 12 more months as the home of baseball's marquee franchise.

"To survive the grind of a 162-game season and the post-season afterwards is something that's hard to measure in terms of how much it takes out of the players," said Canadian Press baseball writer Shi Davidi. "To be able to do it not once, but twice, is really an incredible feat."

The Associated Press/Ed Reinke

BAILEY BEATS THE WORLD IN ATLANTA (1996)

EIGHT YEARS AFTER enduring the worst heartbreak in Canadian Olympic history, fans had a sprint champion they could truly be proud of.

Donovan Bailey didn't care for the comparisons to disgraced runner Ben Johnson. He just wanted to race. And facing the greatest field ever assembled, Bailey was the best of them all, recording a world-record time in the 100-metre final to stake his claim as the fastest man on the planet. The charismatic 28-year-old joined the legendary Percy Williams as the only Canadians to win the marquee race of the Summer Games.

The Canadian Press/COC/Claus Andersen

He would go on to add a second gold in the 4 x 100–metre relay, earning the Lou Marsh Trophy as Canadian Athlete of the Year. Most importantly, Bailey's thrilling performances provided joy, satisfaction, and relief for a country still reeling from the sting of Seoul.

Bailey's metamorphosis into the world's fastest man was rather unconventional. Though Bailey did succeed in track and field after emigrating to Canada from Jamaica as a 13-year-old, he was far more interested in playing basketball. Bailey's love of hoops carried over from his days at Queen Elizabeth Park High School in Oakville, Ont., to his time at Sheridan College, where he earned a degree in business administration. Becoming a professional athlete was the furthest thing from his mind—he preferred the life of a professional stockbroker.

Ever the competitor, Bailey was given some food for thought after watching the 1990 Canadian track and field championships on television. There, Bailey saw the best sprinters the country had to offer, and remembered beating those same sprinters during his high school track days. While he had no intention of giving up his career in the financial sector, Bailey wondered if maybe he could turn some of his attention back to the track. It was a risky venture, but one he was willing to make.

Bailey began running 100-metre dashes on a part-time basis in 1991, and became a member of the national team shortly after. He showed plenty of promise, but struggled to post times that would make him competitive against the world's best sprinters. It wasn't until 1993, when Bailey was spotted by famed American sprinting coach Dan Pfaff, that Bailey's racing career took a drastic turn for the better.

Pfaff invited Bailey to train with him at Louisiana State University, and in 1994, Bailey accepted. Pfaff immediately identified the things Bailey needed to work on the most. Though he was a fast runner, Bailey wasn't yet

a sprinter. His starts were dreadful, and his running style needed plenty of tweaking. Under Pfaff's tutelage, Bailey improved by leaps and bounds, lowering his career-best time by a staggering four-tenths of a second in just one season.

The following year, Bailey completed the transformation from successful stockbroker to world-class sprinter with a pair of emphatic victories. First, Bailey blasted the competition at the Canadian track and field championships, crossing the line in 9.91 seconds—the fastest time of the season, and the greatest-ever performance on Canadian soil. Bailey followed that up with a stunning result at the world championships in Goteborg, Sweden, topping the field in 9.97 seconds. Teammate Bruny Surin finished second in both races, giving Canadian fans a

double dose of sprinting stardom not seen since the days of the disgraced Johnson.

Bailey entered the 1996 Olympic trials in Montreal as the heavy favourite to win. Repeating the form that won him the world title in 1995, Bailey bettered the field with ease, winning the race in 9.98 seconds. The victory stood as a symbol of just how far the Jamaica native had come since committing himself fully to his new career.

Bailey faced waves of expectations from Canadians back home who expected gold—and more than that, they needed gold. It wasn't enough that Bailey had the ghost of Johnson to contend with, he also faced the burden of competing for a country that places enormous value on every medal won at an Olympic Games.

None of it had any effect on Bailey's self-confidence.

"I've never stepped into a race and felt I was in a group with anyone," says Bailey. "I'm a step above them all. I've never been more prepared for an event—it was my race to lose."

Bailey wasn't at his sharpest during his first two races, doing just enough to advance to the final. He ran times of 10.24 and 10.05 seconds, well off his personal best. He contended afterwards that he was saving his best for the following night, when the world's strongest field would convene at Olympic Stadium for the main event of the Games.

Bailey predicted it would take a world-record time to win gold, and many agreed. All eight men in the final field were capable of running a sub-9.9 time. The gold-medal winner would quite likely wind up being the fastest man in history. Bailey believed he was the man for the job.

"I felt I was capable of running in the 9.7s, or even faster," says Bailey. "I had trained so hard for Atlanta. I was prepared to run as fast as it took to win."

The race was plagued by three false starts, including two by Linford Christie, who was disqualified. Christie refused to leave the race area until the referee ushered him away after close to five minutes of complaining. The long delay unnerved Ato Boldon and Frankie Fredericks, both known for their lightning-quick starts. Suddenly, the playing field had been levelled.

Bailey had a decent start, but still found himself well back at the 25-metre mark. What followed was one of the most incredible bursts of natural acceleration in Olympic history. Bailey tore through the field in the middle portion of the race, then caught and passed Fredericks with 20 metres to go. With only Boldin to beat, Bailey maintained his breakneck pace through the finish line before letting out a yelp of celebration. Bailey had become the Olympic champion in a record time of 9.84 seconds.

Bailey draped himself in the Canadian flag after the race, though he pointed out that the victory was as much for his native Jamaica as it was for his adopted homeland, and that suited Canadian fans just fine. Nearly a decade after enduring one of the most disgraceful moments in the history of sport, the country could finally pour its heart out to a 100-metre Olympic champion.

"Everywhere I go, people still remind me about that race," says Bailey. "Canadians are always telling me how much they appreciated my performance. I feel very blessed to have accomplished what I did."

The Canadian Press/Toronto Star/Frank Lennon

CANADA TOPS THE SOVIET UNION IN SUMMIT SERIES (1972)

CANADA SCORED ITS FIRST GOAL of the 1972 Summit Series just 30 seconds into Game 1. Its final tally came with 34 seconds left in Game 8.

The Canadian Press/Peter Bregg

Contained between those scoring plays is one of the greatest exhibitions of hockey the world has ever seen. Canada and the Soviet Union waged a gruelling 480-minute on-ice battle that spanned two continents and thousands of kilometres. There was barbarism and brutality one minute, and breathtaking puck artistry the next. Tensions between the two teams—and the two countries—were as intense as any sporting event in the twentieth century.

And when Canadian forward Paul Henderson found the net behind Soviet netminder Vladislav Tretiak to clinch the series victory for Canada, cheers went up from every corner of the country. Though there was no Stanley Cup title to celebrate or Olympic gold to applaud, fans across the nation knew they had witnessed the greatest moment in Canadian sports history.

"Nobody could repeat the excitement of '72," says hockey legend Wayne Gretzky. "Watching the country rally around the team the way it did, and then seeing the team rally to win ... '72 was easily the best international series Canada has ever had."

Most of the initial focus in Canada wasn't on the eight-game series itself, but rather on which players wouldn't be playing in it. Superstar defenceman Bobby Orr was named to the team, but was told by doctors that he wouldn't be healed in time after undergoing off-season surgery on his left knee. Orr didn't even travel with the club, choosing instead to continue his rehabilitation at his home in Parry Sound, Ont.

The Associated Press

Bobby Hull's exclusion from the Summit Series created considerable controversy after the future Hall-of-Fame forward learned he was ineligible to play unless he signed an NHL contract. Hull had defected to the rival World Hockey Association one month earlier, signing a 10-year mega-deal with the Winnipeg Jets. Even though he had been one of the original invites to Canada's training camp, Hull wouldn't be joining the team.

Despite the two key absences, the series still appeared to be a mismatch on paper. Canada's roster boasted 16 future Hall of Famers, including Boston Bruins scoring sensation Phil Esposito, Philadelphia Flyers agitator Bobby

Clarke, and Montreal Canadiens blue-liner Serge Savard. The goaltending tandem of Montreal's Ken Dryden and Chicago's Tony Esposito was thought to be impenetrable. Fans, media, and even the players and coaches themselves were expecting a blowout.

"I am aiming at winning every game," head coach Harry Sinden said prior to the series. "The boys are very enthusiastic and in much better shape than I expected.

"I wouldn't lose too many games with these guys, even playing regularly in the NHL" (The Canadian Press, August 22, 1972).

The series began as expected, as Esposito and Henderson scored to give the home team a 2–0 lead in the opening six minutes. Once the period reached the halfway point, the Soviets appeared ready to show their Canadian counterparts what they could do.

And they could do plenty.

Evgeny Zimin scored the Soviets' first goal at 11:40. Late in the period, Vladimir Petrov tied the game 2–2. The crowd's enthusiasm waned as the Soviets began dominating play. Their momentum would carry over into the second, when Valeri Kharlamov beat Dryden twice to give the Soviets a 4–2 lead after 40 minutes.

Clarke reduced the deficit early in the third, but Boris Mikhailov restored the two-goal cushion at 13:32. Zimin and Yakushev rounded out the scoring as the Soviets

walloped the Canadians 7–3 in one of the most unexpected outcomes in Canadian hockey history.

Two nights later in Toronto, the Canadians used a new plan of attack: tighten the defence. The tactic worked to perfection in a 4–1 victory that evened the series at a win apiece. Brother acts played a key role in the win, with Phil Esposito scoring Canada's first goal. Younger sibling Tony shut the door in net with a 20-save performance, allowing only Yakushev's second-period power-play goal.

"[Game 1] was a conditioner for us and by the third period [of Game 2] we seemed to be getting over the hump," said Phil Esposito. "After two games now we're pretty close to being in condition and this is going to make a big difference" (The Canadian Press, September 5, 1972).

The Canadians' high was short-lived as they let Game 3 in Winnipeg slip away en route to a 4–4 tie. J.P. Parise and Jean Ratelle had first-period goals to give Canada a 2–1 lead, and Esposito made it a two-goal advantage early in the second. Kharlamov and Henderson exchanged goals 51 seconds apart before Yuri Lebedev and Alexander Bodunov erased the deficit by the end of the second. A scoreless third left the teams even at a win, a loss, and a tie apiece.

Two days later in Vancouver, the Soviets dominated for two periods and cruised to a 5–3 victory that sent boos cascading from the stands. Mikhailov opened with a pair of first-period goals and, after Gilbert Perreault cut the lead early in the second, Yury Blinov and Vladimir Vikulov put the game out of reach later in the period.

Canada headed to the Soviet Union with just one victory in four home games. Talk of Canada's pre-tournament conditioning regimen had been muted—the Soviets were clearly more fit than their counterparts, and were skating circles around the Canadians.

The teams had two weeks to prepare for Game 5, and the break seemed to help Canada immensely. Parise gave his side a 1–0 lead, and Clarke and Henderson extended the advantage in the second. Blinov's goal early in the third made it 3–1, but Henderson's second of the game, moments after crashing into the boards and suffering a concussion, restored the three-goal cushion as fans back home let out a satisfied sigh.

The relief was premature.

Vyacheslav Anasin ignited the comeback at 9:05, and Vladimir Shadrin cut Canada's lead to 4–3 just eight seconds later. Aleksandr Gusev tied the game at 11:41, setting the stage for Vikulov's game-winner at 14:46. Just like that, the Soviets led the series 3–1–1, leaving Canada on the verge of a crushing defeat.

Henderson felt well enough to remain in the lineup despite his concussion, and his presence would define

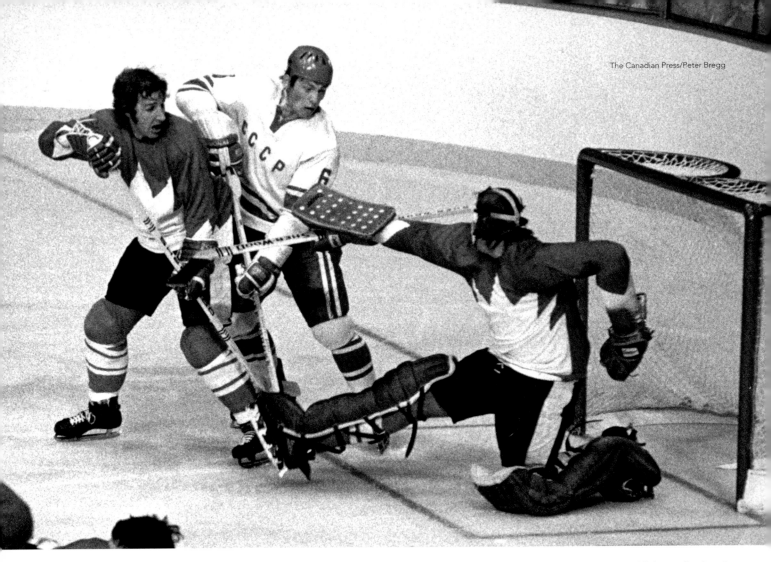

The Canadian Press/Peter Bregg

the rest of the series. Despite spending nearly an entire period of the game short-handed, the Canadians escaped with a 3–2 victory in Game 6 on Henderson's game-winner 6:36 into the second period. The goal came just 15 seconds after Cournoyer had given Canada a 2–1 lead.

With fans and players rejuvenated by the Game 6 victory, Canada eked out a win in Game 7 behind more Henderson heroics. With the score tied 3–3, Henderson slipped past two Soviet defenders and beat Tretiak with 2:06 remaining in the third. Canada and the Soviet Union were now at three wins, three losses, and a tie apiece. The entire series would come down to one final 60-minute showdown.

"[Game 8] might just well be the most exciting game of hockey ever played," Sinden said after Game 7 (The Canadian Press, September 27, 1972).

His words proved prophetic.

Three minutes into the game, Canada found itself down two men when Yakushev opened the scoring. A third straight Canadian penalty, this one to Parise, so enraged the perpetrator that he came within a flash of smashing the referee with his stick. Parise was given a game misconduct for his actions.

Canada calmed down and regained its focus as Esposito tied the score at 6:45. Vladimir Lutchenko and Brad Park traded goals later in the period, making it 2–2 after 20 minutes.

The Soviets broke out in front again on a goal by Vladimir Shadrin just 21 seconds into the second period. Bill White tied it again midway through the period, but goals by Yakushev and Valery Vasiliev gave the Soviets a commanding 5–3 lead after two periods. The Soviets were content to play for the tie; though each team would finish with eight points, the Soviet Union would claim victory by virtue of having scored one more goal than its Canadian opposition.

Esposito gave Canadian fans something to cheer for when his goal at 2:27 cut the lead to 5–4. The Canadians maintained a steady dose of pressure that paid off just over 10 minutes later as Yvon Cournoyer guided a rebound past Tretiak to tie the score.

The Soviets played on their heels from that point on, hoping simply to hang on for a tie. As the game clock ticked away, it appeared they would get their wish. Huddled around radios and television sets, a record Canadian audience crossed its fingers and prayed for any small break that might give its team a chance at victory.

Soon after, the prayers of a nation were answered.

Yvon Cournoyer took control of an errant Soviet pass and attempted a long feed to Henderson, who tripped and slid sideways into the boards. Two Soviet players fumbled with the puck and Esposito snatched it from their grasp.

His weak shot was stopped easily by Tretiak, but the normally unflappable goaltender allowed a rebound, which slid right to Henderson, who was all alone in the front. His first shot attempt hit Tretiak and bounced right back onto his stick. Henderson's second shot tumbled over the outstretched Tretiak, sending the Canadians pouring out onto the ice. With just 34 seconds left, Canada had a 6–5 lead.

The Soviets would not threaten, and a cheer went up from the close to 3,000 Canadian fans in the arena as the team swarmed an elated Dryden. Coaches and trainers embraced on the Canada bench before sliding out to meet the celebrating players. And as both teams met at centre ice to shake hands, the players put their differences behind them, congratulating each other for putting on an unforgettable performance.

The series ended with the playing of "O Canada," during which Canadian players sang, wept, or stood silently, fully aware of the gravity of their victory. Back home, many fans were doing the same. To this day, those fortunate enough to have witnessed the event still remember exactly where they were when Henderson's infamous shot found the net. And despite having a slew of great Olympic results, Stanley Cup victories, Hall of Fame inductions, and record-breaking performances to choose from, no moment in the history of Canadian sport can compare to the one that took place in the Luzhniki Ice Palace in Moscow on September 28, 1972.

HONOURABLE MENTIONS

SOME EVENTS FAILED TO CRACK the Top 100 but were simply too great to leave out. The moments listed in this section may not have earned the votes necessary for inclusion in the main list, but they certainly evoked the kind of emotion and celebration that make them worthy of mention.

SILKEN LAUMANN BATTLES LEG INJURY TO WIN BRONZE (1992)

WHILE IN Germany for a qualifying regatta, Laumann's boat was rammed by a men's pair boat, which severely crushed her leg. Laumann, one of Canada's top medal hopes for the 1992 Olympics in Barcelona later that summer, spent a week in hospital before returning to Canada, her leg so badly damaged that bone was visible. After undergoing five operations to deal with the severe injuries, she immediately resumed training, her lower leg heavily bandaged. Once in Spain, Laumann rowed the race of her life, rallying from fourth place late in the final to surge into bronze-medal position.

CHANTAL PETITCLERC CLEANS UP AT SUMMER GAMES (2004)

PETITCLERC, CANADA'S TOP wheelchair track and field athlete, entered the 2004 Games in Athens with an impressive Olympic resumé: five gold, four silver, and two bronze over three sets of Games. The Quebec City native opened with a decisive victory in the demonstration 800-metre race at the Summer Games. Petitclerc then ratcheted it up several notches at the Paralympics, which followed, setting world records in the 100-metre, 400-metre, and 1,500-metre events. She also set a Paralympic record in her 800-metre victory and added a sixth gold medal for good measure in the 200-metre race.

BRIAN KILREA EARNS 1,000TH CAREER COACHING VICTORY (2003)

AS AN NHL player, Kilrea's career was defined by one moment: scoring the first goal in the history of the Los Angeles Kings franchise in 1967. Kilrea carved out a more memorable niche as a junior hockey coach, beginning in 1974. He led the Ottawa 67's to five division titles and the 1984 Memorial Cup championship in his first stint as coach before heading to the NHL as a New York Islanders assistant. He returned to the 67's two years later, and when Ottawa beat Sudbury 4–2 on March 9, 2003, Kilrea became the first coach in major junior victory to earn 1,000 wins.

ROSS REBAGLIATI RETAINS OLYMPIC GOLD MEDAL (1998)

REBAGLIATI BECAME AN instant fan favourite after capturing the inaugural gold medal in snowboarding at the 1998 Olympics in Nagano, Japan. Controversy ensued when the International Olympic Committee stripped the Vancouver native of his medal after he tested positive for trace amounts of cannabis in a post-race urine test. Rebagliati immediately appealed the decision, and the gold was returned to him after it was determined the IOC rulebook doesn't include marijuana as a banned substance. In his defence, Rebagliati claimed he had ingested second-hand marijuana at a party in Whistler, B.C., prior to the start of the Games.

TORONTO RAPTORS WIN FIRST-EVER PLAYOFF SERIES (2001)

THE BEGINNING OF the twenty-first century represented a fresh start for the Toronto Raptors. The franchise's first three years of existence yielded plenty of negativity and despair, and precious few victories. Things changed in the 1999–2000 season, when the team finished with a franchise-record 45 wins and a first-ever playoff berth. A three-game sweep at the hands of the New York Knicks left players and fans alike with a bad taste, but it wouldn't last long. Behind another all-star season from superstar Vince Carter, the Raps reeled off 47 regular-season wins in 2000–01 before disposing of the rival Knicks in five games for the first series victory in franchise history.

CAROLYN WALDO WINS DOUBLE GOLD IN SYNCHRO (1988)

WALDO ARRIVED in Seoul with high hopes after capturing a solo silver medal at the 1984 Summer Games in Los Angeles. She and Michelle Cameron were also expected to do well in the duet competition, having won a number of high-profile events, including the 1985 FINA World Cup and the 1986 Commonwealth Games. Korea wound up being doubly lucrative for Waldo, who beat American Tracie Ruiz to win the solo event before teaming with Cameron to capture the duet. Waldo became the first Canadian woman to win multiple golds at a single Games, earning her the Lou Marsh Award as Canadian athlete of the year.

MIKE PRINGLE RUSHES FOR 2,000 YARDS IN A SEASON (1998)

DANIEL NESTOR UPSETS WORLD NO. 1 STEFAN EDBERG (1992)

A STUNNING five-set victory against the world's top player propelled Nestor onto the international tennis scene. Armed with a booming serve, the 19-year-old surprised his Swedish opponent in their Davis Cup tie. After dropping the first set 6–4, Nestor battled back to win the second set 6–3. He struggled mightily in the third set, losing 6–1, but showed poise beyond his years against the six-time Grand Slam champion, upending Edberg 6–3 in the fourth set. With the Vancouver crowd cheering every Nestor point, the lanky lefty did the improbable, capturing the final set 6–4 to conclude the biggest upset in Canadian tennis history.

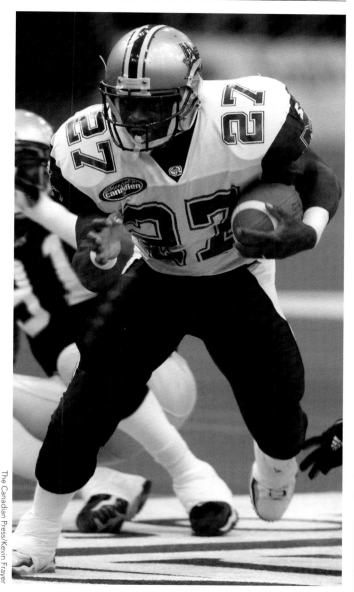

The Canadian Press/Kevin Frayer

The Canadian Press/Jacques Boissinot

WITH THE NFL ultimately uninterested in his services, Pringle had to settle for being one of the CFL's greatest rushers. Pringle exploded onto the scene in 1994 with 1,972 rushing yards, helping the Baltimore CFLers reach their first Grey Cup. A 1,700-yard effort the following season led to an invitation from the Denver Broncos, where he was a late cut from training camp. Pringle then headed to Montreal where, in his second full season with the Alouettes, he became the first CFL player to amass 2,000 rushing yards in a season. He finished with 2,065 yards that season, taking home his second Most Outstanding Player award.

ANNE HEGGTVEIT WINS CANADA'S FIRST OLYMPIC SKI GOLD (1960)

AT A TIME WHEN downhill skiing was dominated by Europeans, Heggtveit was the first Canadian to break up the monopoly in Olympic competition. Encouraged by teammate Lucille Wheeler's downhill and giant slalom triumphs at the 1958 world championships, Heggtveit wowed the crowd at Squaw Valley, Calif., winning the Olympic slalom event by a whopping three seconds over runner-up Betsy Snite of the U.S. The unexpected gold medal made the Ottawa native an instant hero back home, where she captured the Lou Marsh Award as Canadian Athlete of the Year. She would also serve as the inspiration for future Canadian gold medallists like Nancy Greene and Kerrin Lee-Gartner.

The Canadian Press/COC

JEFF BUTTLE PLAYS WORLD-BEATER TO END CANADIAN DROUGHT (2008)

The Canadian Press/Paul Chiasson

MANY OBSERVERS FELT that Buttle had reached his figure-skating peak at the 2006 Olympic Games in Turin, Italy, where he won the bronze medal in men's singles. As it turned out, Buttle had plenty more in the tank. The native of Smooth Rock Falls, Ont., dazzled audiences at the world championship in Göteborg, Sweden, despite entering the competition as an overwhelming underdog. He captured both the short and long programs, trouncing runner-up Brian Joubert of France by nearly 14 points while earning Canada's first men's world championship in 11 years.

ACKNOWLEDGEMENTS

THERE WOULDN'T HAVE BEEN a book without the help of the voting panel. A special thank you to the contributors: Chris Cuthbert, Stephen Brunt, Martine Gaillard, James Duthie, Dave Feschuk, Sean Fitzgerald, Derek Snider, Shi Davidi, Gregory Strong, Dan Ralph, Dan McGinty, Gavin MacKenzie, Eric Koreen, Bob Coatsworth, Jonathan Bliangas, Joe Ross, and Curtis Withers.

I also want to thank all of the athletes, coaches, and reporters who provided interviews, and all of the media and public relations directors who helped set up the interviews and put up with my endless barrage of e-mails and phone calls along the way.

Additional thanks go to Charles Messina, Thuy Anh Nguyen, and Patti Tasko from The Canadian Press for helping me take a small idea and turn it into something big.

Lastly, I would like to thank my family, friends, and co-workers, without whom none of this would have been possible. There are too many to name, but they all know who they are—and what they've meant to me along the way. Thanks, all.

COVER PHOTO CREDITS

45. The Canadian Press
46. The Associated Press
47. The Canadian Press/Frank Gunn
48. The Canadian Press
49. The Canadian Press/Globe and Mail/ Tom Szlukovenyi
50. The Canadian Press/Dave Buston
51. The Canadian Press/David Eulitt
52. The Canadian Press
53. The Canadian Press/Hans Deryk
54. The Canadian Press/COC/Ted Grant
55. The Canadian Press/Tom Hanson
56. The Canadian Press/Chuck Stoody
57. The Canadian Press/Michael Creagan
58. The Canadian Press/COC
59. The Canadian Press/Andrew Vaughan
60. The Associated Press/Michael Conroy
61. The Canadian Press/Montreal Gazette
62. The Associated Press/Mary Butkus
63. The Canadian Press/Montreal Star
64. The Canadian Press/COC/Andrè Forget
65. The Canadian Press
66. The Canadian Press/COC/Cromby McNeil
67. The Canadian Press/Jacques Boissinot
68. The Canadian Press/London Free Press
69. The Associated Press/Elaine Thompson
70. The Canadian Press/Globe and Mail
71. The Canadian Press/Chris Bolin
72. The Associated Press
73. The Canadian Press/COC/Claus Andersen
74. The Canadian Press/COC
75. The Canadian Press/COC/Sandy Grant
76. The Canadian Press/Doug Ball
77. The Canadian Press/COC/O. Bierwagon
78. The Canadian Press/Ryan Remiorz
79. The Associated Press/Ray Stubblebine
80. The Associated Press/Matt York
81. The Canadian Press/Richard Lam
82. The Canadian Press/Toronto Star/Jeff Goode
83. The Canadian Press
84. The Canadian Press/Dave Buston
85. The Canadian Press/Paul Chiasson
86. The Canadian Press/Frank Gunn
87. The Canadian Press/National Archives of Canada
88. The Canadian Press/John Lehmann
89. The Canadian Press/Ryan Remiorz
90. The Canadian Press/COC/Ted Grant
91. The Canadian Press//Edmonton Sun/Christine Vanzella
92. The Canadian Press/Dave Buston
93. La Presse Canadienne/AOC/Andrè Forget
94. The Associated Press/Gene J. Puskar
95. The Canadian Press/Toronto Star/Frank Lennon
96. The Associated Press/David Guttenfelder
97. The Canadian Press/Edmonton Sun/Brendon Dlouhy
98. The Canadian Press/Boris Spremo
99. The Canadian Press/Chuck Stoody
100. The Canadian Press/Montreal Gazette

101. The Canadian Press/Paul Chiasson
102. The Associated Press/Elise Amendola
103. The Associated Press/ Dusan Vranic
104. The Canadian Press/Dave Buston
105. The Canadian Press
106. The Canadian Press/COC
107. The Canadian Press/Mark J. Terrill
108. The Canadian Press/Edmonton Journal/Brian Gavriloff

1. The Canadian Press/Blaise Edwards
2. The Associated Press/Hans Deryk
3. The Canadian Press/Chuck Stoody
4. The Associated Press/Dusan Vranic
5. The Canadian Press/Chuck Stoody
6. The Associated Press/Reed Saxon
7. The Canadian Press/COC
8. The Associated Press
9. The Canadian Press/Andre Pichette
10. The Associated Press/Ben Margot
11. The Associated Press/Keith Srakocic
12. The Canadian Press
13. The Associated Press/Kathy Willens
14. The Associated Press/Paul Sancya
15. The Associated Press/Elise Amendola
16. The Canadian Press/Paul Chiasson
17. The Canadian Press/COC
18. The Canadian Press/Jonathan Hayward
19. The Associated Press/Craig Fujii
20. The Canadian Press/Ryan Remiorz
21. The Canadian Press/COC
22. The Canadian Press

23. The Canadian Press
24. The Canadian Press/Doug Ball
25. The Canadian Press/COC/Mike Ridewood
26. The Associated Press
27. The Canadian Press/Dave Buston
28. The Associated Press/Mark Duncan
29. The Canadian Press
30. The Canadian Press/Chuck Stoody
31. The Canadian Press/Andrew Vaughan
32. The Canadian Press/COC
33. The Canadian Press/COC/J. Merrithew
34. The Canadian Press/Jon Murray
35. The Canadian Press/Ryan Remiorz
36. The Canadian Press/Toronto Star/Jeff Goode
37. The Associated Press/Roy Dabner
38. The Canadian Press/Ryan Remiorz
39. The Associated Press/David Zalubowski
40. The Associated Press/Charlie Riedel
41. The Canadian Press/Kevin Frayer
42. The Canadian Press/Frank Gunn
43. The Associated Press/John J. Lent
44. The Canadian Press/Kevin Frayer